MW01688184

FIT FOR LOVE

Find your self and your perfect mate

by

Olga Sheean

Inside Out Media

Published in Canada, 2005, by Inside Out Media
fitforlove@insideoutmedia.net

Design and illustrations by Lewis Evans
www.lewisevans.net

Library and Archives Canada Cataloguing in Publication

Sheean, Olga, 1959-
Fit for love : find your self and your perfect mate / written by Olga Sheean ; illustrations by Lewis Evans.

ISBN 0-9738222-1-X (bound) ISBN 0-9738222-0-1 (spiral binding)

1. Mate selection. 2. Interpersonal relations. 3. Self-actualization (Psychology). I. Title.

HQ801.S528 2005 306.7 C2005-902899-8

To my parents,
for their unfailing love and support

and to Lew,
who is living proof that all things are possible

All disease, all discomfort is the result of an opinion—
in essence, a lie individuals believe about themselves or their life.
Find the lie for them, tell them the truth and you've given back their health.
The truth is always the cure.

—Dr Phineas Parkhurst Quimby, 1802-1866,
father of the New Thought movement

contents

Preface 6
Introduction: are you fit for love? 8

Part I **How we grow as individuals and how dysfunction develops 13**
1. The foundation of self 14
2. Relating—the story of your life 18

Part II **Solutions and techniques for creating what we want, overcoming key areas of dysfunction, and healing old wounds so that we are free to be more fully ourselves 21**
3. Triggers and their emotional charge 22
4. Filling in the missing pieces 28
   Acceptance 30
   Trust 36
   Authenticity 44
   Intimacy 46
   Other missing pieces 49

Part III **Exploring relationship dynamics; practical tools for living a life of healthy balance and conscious choice 53**
5. Living in the grey zone—where love lies in limbo 54
6. The neediness cycle 60
7. Feeding the need 66
8. The compensation factor—our emotional 'first-aid kit' 70
9. Looking for evidence 76
10. The limitations of labelling 78
11. Focus and projection—reality perspectives 82
12. The power-struggle syndrome 86
13. Subtexts—reading between the lines 96
14. Parental payback—our emotional weaponry 102

Part IV **Growing and evolving in our relationships; troubleshooting techniques to help prevent us from falling back into old patterns and beliefs 107**
15. Going deeper 108
16. Meaningful marriage 114
17. Using your unique gifts 118
18. Troubleshooting 126
19. The 10 Commitments—a code of consciousness for a fulfilling life 130

Preface

Love is safe when you know how to use it.

—Barbara de Angelis

Intimacy can be a scary prospect. If we were really honest with ourselves, most of us who have been through a few relationships would probably admit that it is what we most want in life, yet most fear. We know that relationships have the potential to bring us happiness, but we also know that they can result in heartache and even bitter lawsuits that strip us of everything we own. It's an emotional gamble, enough to give pause to even the sturdiest of hearts. But scarier still is the fact that we seem to be unable to control or predict the outcome.

But is that really so? What if, in fact, we were very much in control of what happens to us, but simply were unaware of how or when we do that? This question took me on a wondrous journey of discovery and adventure, whose ultimate destination did not exist on any map. It was a place buried deep within, and covered over with layers of conditioning and false beliefs that had prevented me from seeing and applying a very powerful truth. It was a place of understanding that yielded startling insights into how the universe actually works—and how we individually work within it.

To reach that understanding, however, I took the long way around, trekking across continents in an attempt to somehow escape my own unhappiness, only to come face to face with myself at each new destination. Everywhere I went, there I was, no wiser or more fulfilled than before.

On my journeys, I observed different cultures and lifestyles and tried to figure out why all my relationships had gone so horribly wrong. In some of the poorest rural communities of Latin America, I crossed paths with shamans, healers and spiritual teachers—simple, ordinary people who were closely connected to the earth and offered timely wisdom for lost travellers like myself. Intent on surviving from day to day, without the distractions of Western-style consumerism, these people focused on supporting and loving each other. Their relationships with family and friends formed the fabric of their existence and, sometimes, made the difference between life and death. Despite their extreme poverty, they never complained. The dignity of the human spirit was evident in their silent humility. I knew that such acceptance had to come from somewhere deep inside and I yearned for the same kind of inner peace.

Tired of chasing myself around the globe, I decided it was time for a new approach—

something that would take me beyond my conscious self and somehow make sense of my life. I began studying mind-body-integration techniques and applied kinesiology—a diagnostic tool that can be used to tap into the subconscious mind to find out what is going on inside, physically, mentally, emotionally and spiritually. This was a very different kind of journey—one of self-discovery, healing and personal empowerment (which ultimately brought me face to face with my true self *and* my ideal mate). I began to see certain patterns emerging, which seemed to be universally applicable, and I finally understood why my own life had been such a mess.

Inside each of us is heaven and hell, differentiated only by our beliefs. It is these that separate us from each other—and from ourselves. Many of them are subconscious negative beliefs that prevent us from seeing what is right in front of our eyes or from understanding our own emotions. We do not see the pain that often lies behind anger, the yearning for love behind detachment, or the creative spontaneity buried beneath our daily routine at work. We need an 'emotional dictionary' to translate the unfathomable foreign 'languages' that we speak to each other in the form of mind games, body language and all the other survival strategies that we have learned along the way in order to hide a part of ourselves that we believe is unacceptable. And we need the willingness to believe that there is one common language of the heart that can bring us together in true intimacy.

Through this unifying language of the heart, we can come to understand the depth and power of each individual, and what it is that blocks its honest expression.

Fit for Love is designed to help you figure out who you really are inside and how to master the language of love so that you can relate to yourself and others with honesty, authenticity and passion. It is a guide to using relationships as a pathway to personal empowerment and spiritual integration.

In considering the principles described in this book, you may feel resistance to believing in them. You may dismiss them straight away, before you even put them to the test for yourself. Or you may be so convinced that your life is beyond your control that you see no point in trying to change anything. Unless your desire for a better life is stronger than your limiting beliefs, your fears will win and you may never know what you could have achieved. But if you are willing to wholeheartedly apply the principles described in this book, you will discover a powerful side to yourself that you may never have experienced. Love and fulfillment will start to permeate your life and you will begin to see magic happen. You will also become aware of your tremendous ability to positively influence your world, to express your unique creativity, and to experience your ultimate self.

There is no greater journey.

Are you fit for love?

Love—or the lack of it—shapes our lives. How deeply we dig for it, how much we believe in it, and how we apply it in our lives, determines our success in finding emotional, financial and spiritual fulfillment. We were put on this earth collectively so that we could learn how to love and understand each other—through each other. Coming here one at a time or living alone in a remote cave would not serve our purpose of self-realization.

Relationships fail because of our incomplete understanding of their true purpose as stepping-stones to personal empowerment. They are powerful catalysts for change and they challenge us to rise above whatever might be in the way of love and our authentic self-expression. In mastering the art of intimate relationship, we ultimately reach a place of deep inner peace and acceptance. Providing us with a unique perspective of ourselves, relationships can show us what is missing within and they can help us to make ourselves complete.

We are all worthy of love, but many of us do not deem ourselves fit to receive it. Getting 'fit for love' is one of the most rewarding fitness programmes we can ever undertake. It is a programme with numerous hidden benefits and extras. It may involve using some new muscles and doing some painful stretches. It may mean forcing ourselves to do the exercises even when they are difficult or unpleasant. But if we stick with the programme and get ourselves fit, we will not only attract love and fulfillment into our lives, but also more breakthroughs and miracles than we could ever have dreamed of when we signed up.

Do you feel unfit for love? Are you tired of trying to make your relationships work or find the ideal partner? Do you feel powerless to change your life for the better? Do you feel unfulfilled? If so, this book is for you.

If you are willing to explore some deeper parts of yourself, this book will take you somewhere new and exciting. It will give you the tools to break out of any self-defeating cycles and transform your life. The techniques described here are effective and universally valid, but transforming your self in the face of resistance—both your own and that of those around you—requires commitment and a strong desire for a better life.

Because dysfunction usually develops over time, we often fail to recognize it for what it is. In that respect, humans are a bit like frogs. If you put a frog in hot water, it will immediately jump out. But if you put it in cold water and slowly heat it up, the frog will not try to escape. Likewise, dysfunction creeps up on us slowly, with beliefs and expectations laid down in childhood and gradually cemented as we grow. Often we do not realize that our dysfunctional lives are not the norm or that things could be any different. So we stay put—in unfulfilling or even abusive relationships, in mind-numbingly unrewarding jobs, or in the empty routine of a solitary existence. We do not realize that we have the power to change things, since we usually do not believe that we could possibly have created our situation in the first place.

When confronted with the possibility of change, many of us baulk. Change means breaking free of the familiar and risking the rejection or ridicule of others. Change means opening up to something new and abandoning the familiar landmarks that we associate with safety, security and predictability. But change is as inevitable as the aging of our bodies and the transition of one season to the other, and security is a myth that not even the tightest insurance policy can dispel. We may be able to protect ourselves financially, but nothing can protect us from the biggest threat of all—our subconscious minds. Less of a computer than an old bunker, our mind contains an arsenal of unstable time bombs, all too readily detonated by particular events, circumstances or emotions. Our mind runs our body. And rarely do we question the validity of what our mind tells us because we think it is on our side. We believe it is there to serve us, and to be our ally, whereas, in fact, it is often the biggest traitor we are likely to meet. Unless positively programmed from an early age, it puts more stock in other people's opinions than in what we ourselves have to say. It defers to those outside us, rather than listening to our inner wisdom. And it leads us to believe that it is far safer and more beneficial not to confront our fears than to meet them head on and perhaps do something extra-ordinary. Our minds create complex strategies designed to keep us from seeing our true selves and, unless we are prepared to do some serious detective work, we are unlikely to ever learn the full truth about who we are. As a result, we are the ultimate undercover operators, assuming a role we were taught as children, yet blissfully ignorant of our own deception and of our own potential greatness.

But if our minds are so clever, how can we find out what we need in order to access our deeper, more authentic selves? How can we be sure that a better life is possible or that anything we do can make a difference?

This book will help you find the answers to these questions.

Part I explains how we grow as individuals and how dysfunction develops.

Part II provides solutions and techniques for creating what we want and overcoming key areas of dysfunction; it helps us heal the wounds of the past, freeing us up to be more fully ourselves.

Part III looks at other aspects of relationship dynamics and provides practical tools for living a life of healthy balance and conscious choice.

Part IV explores ways of going deeper in our relationships; it contains troubleshooting techniques to help prevent us from falling back into old patterns and beliefs so that we can continue to grow and evolve.

Filling out the questionnaire on the following page will give you an idea of what you stand to gain from getting—and staying—'fit for love'.

The Fit for Love *questionnaire*

Tick as appropriate

		Yes	No
1.	Have you recently been, or are you currently, in a relationship in which you felt/feel abused, disrespected, unacceptable or unimportant?	☐	☐
2.	Have any of your former relationships ended in an unfriendly or hurtful way?	☐	☐
3.	Are you seeking the ideal partner but are no longer sure that he/she exists?	☐	☐
4.	Do you dislike being alone?	☐	☐
5.	Do you ever suffer from depression or inexplicable sadness?	☐	☐
6.	Do you ever feel numb inside or devoid of feeling?	☐	☐
7.	Do you suffer from headaches, intestinal problems or other chronic conditions?	☐	☐
8.	Do you often feel tired for no apparent reason?	☐	☐
9.	Do you indulge in comfort foods when you are feeling down?	☐	☐
10.	Are you stressed by, or unhappy with, your job or work environment?	☐	☐
11.	Do you frequently have arguments with your partner, family, friends or colleagues?	☐	☐
12.	Do you feel as if you have no control over your life?	☐	☐
13.	Do you dream of a different life but cannot see how to make it happen?	☐	☐
14.	Do you feel as if your gifts or talents are not being fully utilized?	☐	☐
15.	Do you make snap judgements of people, based on who you think they are?	☐	☐
16.	Are there things that you avoid doing or saying because you fear others' reactions?	☐	☐
17.	Do you berate or criticize yourself if you do something wrong or stupid?	☐	☐
18.	Do you sometimes over-react to certain people who annoy or intimidate you?	☐	☐
19.	Do you avoid conflict, if at all possible?	☐	☐
20.	Do you ever feel that your opinion does not count, or that your input would not make a difference?	☐	☐

Power points

If you answered NO to every question: you do not need this book. You are fully empowered as an individual and are on track with your purpose. You are authentic and true to yourself, and do not compromise yourself for the sake of others. Your mind is strong and healthy, and this is reflected in your body. You make wise choices based on the present moment, having healed any wounds from the past.

If you answered YES to 1–5 of the questions: with a little bit of work, you can get powerfully back on track. Enhancing your self-confidence and self-worth will enable you to make the necessary choices to move forward. See Chapter 4 on filling in your 'missing pieces' and do the accompanying exercise. See Chapter 12 on the power-struggle syndrome for tips on how you can more consciously use your personal power. Chapters 15 (Going deeper), 17 (Using your unique gifts) and 18 (Troubleshooting) may also help you to explore more of your potential and ensure that you do not fall back into old patterns.

If you answered YES to 6–10 of the questions: there is a great deal of power within you that is not being used. You are likely to feel uncomfortable in your body, with some physical symptoms of disease, and may tend not to put yourself first in your own life. Confidence, acceptance, trust and respect are likely to be some of your missing pieces, with several aspects of your life being based on compromise and meeting the needs of others. You would benefit greatly from most of the tools and practical tips on how to reconnect with your power and break out of self-defeating cycles. If you diligently apply the principles in this book and do the accompanying exercises, you can make positive, lasting changes in your life.

If you answered YES to 11–20 of the questions: your power has been severely suppressed and your body and mind have suffered. You are probably unhappy with life and are likely to have some health challenges as well as low energy levels. You have yet to explore your true purpose and value in life, and a great deal of your energy is probably being used up by taking care of others' needs and dealing with your own fears or self-doubts. You may find it hard to make decisions and tend to second-guess yourself frequently. Others may seem to have control over you and you may find it difficult to override them and make a stand for yourself. You have probably had numerous disappointments and do not think you are capable of living the kind of life you may once have dreamed of. Every chapter in this book will be of benefit if you are willing to trust that change is possible and if you do the exercises faithfully. If you choose to do that, you have the means to find happiness and to break free of some crippling cycles that have kept you stuck all your life.

Part I

How we grow as individuals and how dysfunction develops

Chapter 1

The foundation of self

Remember that you are this universe, and this universe is you.
—Joy Harjo

There is one all-powerful force in your life with which you do daily battle. It is not gravity, time, illness, your partner, your in-laws, or your job. It is you.

Although life may appear to be a form of random chaos beyond our control, our world is very powerfully determined by the way we subconsciously relate to ourselves. And how we relate to ourselves is determined by the many fears and beliefs we acquire at an early age. Our need to survive leads us to develop defence mechanisms and compensation strategies designed to help us cope with a world that seems to just 'happen'. However, these reactive strategies can create self-defeating cycles that prevent us from getting what we want.

We may find ourselves repeating the same kind of dysfunctional relationship—for example, grappling with issues of disrespect or poor communication. We may go from one dissatisfying job to another, unable to find meaningful work. Or we may get angry with certain people who trigger some unresolved issue within us. In all cases, we are falling short of our potential for personal fulfillment. We are also being distracted from the real source of power. For if we blame others for what is happening in our lives, then we are giving them control over the situation. True personal power comes from acknowledging our responsibility—and our right—to shape our own destiny.

As children, we depend on our parents to provide us with a solid foundation upon which to build our sense of self. Love, support and encouragement build a positive, stable foundation, infusing us with confidence and a sense of our place in the world. But if those formative, nurturing qualities are insufficient for our particular needs, our foundation is shaky and we lack that inner security and sense of belonging. Regardless of how we are treated as adults, our primary relationship with our parents forms the foundation of our personality and the dynamics of all future relationships.

By exploring what is missing from our foundation, we can gain an understanding of why certain elements are missing from our life. We can then repair and strengthen the foundation, filling in the cracks so that it supports our dreams, goals and purpose.

To do this requires taking responsibility for our life. It also requires an openness to the possibility that we are powerful enough to have attracted certain dynamics in our life—good and bad—in order to learn just how very powerful we are. Breaking out of our self-defeating cycles, then, may involve a shift towards a new way of thinking; it may require a perspective that will demonstrate our tremendous personal power. Finally, it requires making a choice to change and evolve, based on the recognition that we are uniquely responsible for our own life.

We are constantly faced with choices in life. They make life exciting and dynamic, but they also enable us to exercise our power. The most fundamental of choices we make is the way we choose to perceive life itself. We live in a world of duality—of opposites, such as hot and cold, yes and no, acceptance and rejection. Similarly, we can either react to life coming at us, or we can proactively influence our world through our thoughts, words and actions.

True personal power comes from acknowledging our responsibility —and our right—to shape our own destiny.

If we opt for merely coping with life, by avoiding, reacting to, or surviving whatever comes our way, we tend to lead a life of reaction and defence, which often generates frustration, disillusionment and, ultimately, cynicism. As life continues to 'come at us', we can become resigned to expecting the worst, and often get it. This serves as further proof that life does, indeed, just 'happen', and we may see ourselves as victims, powerless to make a difference.

Knowing that we can make a difference transforms the way we live. Those who believe in their power as individuals can live a life of creative self-responsibility,

which ultimately leads to a state of inner peace and love. They see life's challenges as a means of developing their formidable power as human beings. They may also appreciate the purpose of duality, knowing that one can only fully experience unconditional love if one first experiences the lack of it.

Many of us prefer to continue blaming others for what is not working in our lives, rather than assuming personal responsibility for it. This is a choice we are free to make. However, it is unlikely to bring us any great personal fulfillment, and may leave us feeling resentful and disappointed later in life.

If we choose the path of personal empowerment, we become aware of the power and responsibility that go with that choice. In using that responsibility wisely, we can live a life of higher meaning. We will also become aware of the survival techniques that we have developed in reaction to life's challenges. Only when we can see how we have tried to compensate for deficiencies of love in our life, and devised protective measures to avoid being hurt, can we begin to break out of our self-defeating cycles.

By understanding our subconscious, we can apply practical techniques with which to consciously orchestrate our life. This puts us back where we belong—powerfully on track with our talents, purpose and dreams. It also gives us the means to be happy.

Imagine living a life of total solitude,
without any interaction with other human beings.

Would you have any idea of who you were?

Chapter 2

Relating: the story of your life

Our relationship to self determines our relationship to others.

Life is essentailly a process of relating—to self, to others, to the world around us. We need others in our lives to show us who we are and who we can become. Without them, we would have no one to react to, compete with, be jealous of, encourage, support or love. We would have no means of experiencing the full range of human emotions, as triggered or inspired by those around us.

Whether we are relating to our partner, employer, friend or lawyer, we are always in some form of relationship. And *how* we relate to the world determines how it relates back to us. The solutions to our conflicts with others come from understanding and resolving our inner conflicts, and relationships provide the key to this process of discovery and reconciliation.

To 'relate' to another is to tell that person something—like relating or recounting a story. The 'story' we tell is about ourselves, and it is transmitted through our thoughts, fears, beliefs, expectations, words and actions. As physical beings with an electromagnetic field and a highly-developed central nervous system, we are broadcasting and receiving information every moment of our existence. Our electrical field and cellular memory are filled with electrical and emotional charges relating to our life experiences, and they tell their own story independently of our verbal communication. This communication network is in constant interaction with the outside world, reacting to stimuli, filtering information, and generally acting as a radar system for our physical selves.

Through our energy field, we broadcast messages based on who we think we are and what we perceive to be our place in the world. Our beliefs and perceptions take shape in our formative years (ages one to seven), during which time we come to certain conclusions about our 'lovability' or worthiness, based on how we are treated by others.

Sheila, for example, was born to reserved, conservative parents who were uncomfortable expressing open affection or warmth. As a result, she came to the conclusion that she did not deserve to be loved and was therefore unlovable. From this basic assumption, she also concluded that she was not good enough and, by the time she was 30, had developed low self-esteem, shyness and a need to give to others in an attempt to earn love in return. She was overly sensitive and had difficulty in receiving, despite her good looks and sharp mind. When Sheila's heart shut down because of insensitive parenting, the energy that would normally have gone towards emotionally-motivated endeavours was instead channelled into her mental faculties. This led to enhanced intelligence and a mental acuity that Sheila used in an attempt to avoid any further 'threat' to her safety. She became highly skilled at protecting herself, but had little practice in loving. Though her heightened intelligence and emotional detachment served her well in her business, she was empty and unfulfilled in her relationships.

Thus begins the formation of our 'missing pieces'—those elements of emotional nourishment that we most needed early in life but did not get (see Chapter 4). These missing pieces lead to the development of destructive cycles or patterns that defeat us in our attempts to find happiness. They build the foundation for a lifetime of struggle and self-rejection.

Our external world always reflects back to us what is going on inside at a deeper, subconscious level. This is usually the only way we realize that something is missing within us. Without that external mirror, we would have difficulty seeing ourselves. When we are missing certain forms of emotional nourishment, we therefore attract situations and relationships that lack these same emotional elements.

These components will continue to be missing in our lives—and to be reflected back to us—until we learn how to provide them for ourselves. This is why relationships can sometimes be extremely frustrating. They act as our personal mirrors and sounding boards, challenging us to make ourselves complete. If we do not understand this, however, our partners will continue to trigger us, causing us to react in ways that perpetuate our cycles and stop us from getting what we have been missing all along.

The beginning of distortion

Parental love forms the foundation upon which we construct our self-identity, personal security and our sense of belonging in the world. If we feel deprived of that love, we need to fill the emotional void with something else. Whatever we receive instead of this formative love, then, provides that foundation. If, instead of experiencing unconditional love, we feel neglected, we quickly translate this feeling into the belief that we are unlovable. This belief then becomes the inverted tip of the pyramid upon which all else in life is subsequently constructed (see illustration below). As soon as we develop these self-limiting beliefs, they are stored in our subconscious and begin to be transmitted to the outside world.

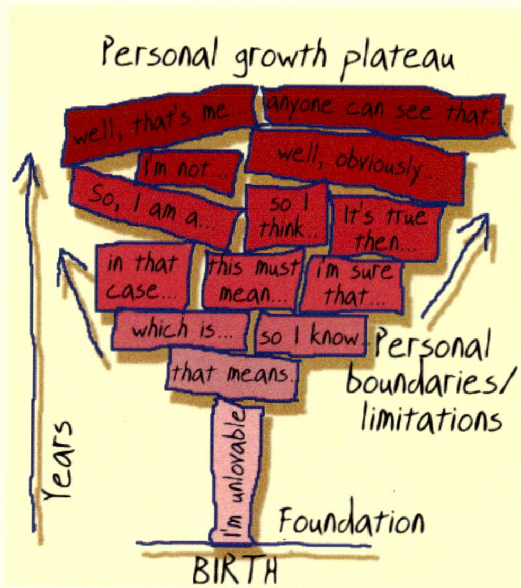

Part II

Solutions and techniques for creating what we want, overcoming key areas of dysfunction, and healing old wounds so that we are free to be more fully ourselves

Chapter 3

Triggers and their emotional charge

If you are not operating 'free of charge', you are probably costing yourself a fortune.

Triggers are areas of sensitivity relating to some former painful experience. They have an emotional charge behind them and cause us to react instinctively when they are activated.

Triggers relate to some form of disempowerment and are the motivational devices used by the subconscious to drive us towards reclaiming that thwarted power. They are the conclusions we come to about ourselves, as a result of the way we were treated as children. Usually of the 'I'm-not-good-enough' variety, they are also the driving forces behind our cycles (i.e., patterns that keep repeating themselves in our lives, seemingly beyond our control). By a simple process of objective self-examination, we can identify our dominant trigger among the following:

powerless/weak unlovable
not good enough/unacceptable
wrong/stupid no value/worthless
insignificant/unimportant

Identify something that upsets you—for example, being manipulated or controlled by your partner or employer. Then ask yourself what kind of person would be manipulated or controlled in this way. Your answer may be, "Someone who is weak or powerless". If you are always afraid of voicing your opinion, ask yourself what kind of person would be afraid of that. Your answer may be, "Someone who has nothing important to say". Now ask yourself what kind of person would have nothing important to say, and you may come up with something similar to the 'no value/worthless' trigger.

Triggers are not necessarily the result of deep trauma or significant painful incidents in one's life. They can just as easily become rooted in our subconscious as a result of one harsh word, a simple oversight on the part of an over-stressed parent, or by someone's neglect of our needs.

To understand our triggers, we first need to identify the driving forces behind them: fear, habit, beliefs, memories and need or dependence.

The three degrees of **fear** are the most powerful driving forces in the development of our triggers. *Defensiveness* is our protective reaction to some perceived threat. It prompts us to argue, justify or validate as a means of coping when a sensitive issue—or trigger—is activated. *Avoidance* is a decision we make (consciously or subconsciously) so that we do not have to deal with the threat or our reactions to it. *Denial* is when we delude ourselves by saying, for example, that it is not because we are *afraid* that we are avoiding doing something, it is simply because we do not *want* to do it.

A **habit** is something so engrained that we do it without thinking. It is encoded in our subconscious, like driving a car or riding a bicycle, and therefore needs to become conscious before it can be broken down into its composite parts and transformed into a new approach.

Beliefs can encompass the full range of human potential, from 'I'm a genius', to 'I'm utterly worthless', and all the gradations in between. If our beliefs are of the limiting variety, they inhibit us in the fulfillment of our dreams, relationships and purpose. They cause us to make detours in life—to travel a long, uphill, winding path rather than the straight, easy road to success. Or they can lead to complete inaction—a paralysis generated entirely by our mind. In almost all cases, we take up where our parents or other role models left off, perpetuating whatever beliefs they implanted in us.

Memories are images that, if painful, can have a powerful emotional charge behind them. They are like little time bombs, intermittently activated by association or similar circumstance. They can be powerful 'pre-programmers', creating expectations based on our worst fears and backed by seemingly sound evidence.

Need or dependence stems from what is missing within us—those emotional qualities and nourishment we lacked in childhood. They can generate expectations, resentment, power struggles, and co-dependent relationships in which no one gets what they want. Needing a partner to help you make decisions is just one example of how this can occur. (See Chapter 6: 'The neediness cycle'.)

There are five major factors involved in not getting what we want out of life:

Fear, *leading to defensiveness, avoidance and/or denial*

Habit, *leading to an automatic, repetitive way of doing things*

Beliefs, *leading to limitation, deviation or inaction*

Memories, *leading to projection of the past into the future*

Need/dependence, *leading to being stuck, 'against our will'*

The following two exercises will enable you to identify the driving forces behind your particular triggers.

Exercise 1

List your main fears, most destructive habits, most limiting beliefs, any memories that haunt or hinder you, and any areas of need or dependence on others.

Fears:
e.g.: I'm afraid my partner will leave me

Habits:
e.g.: I always make jokes when I'm nervous

Negative beliefs:
e.g.: I think I'm unattractive

Bad memories
e.g.: I remember being intimidated by a gang at school

Needs/dependence:
e.g.: I need my partner to help me make decisions.

Now that you have identified some of your fears, beliefs, habits, memories and needs, you can determine the most dominant triggers in your life. Doing this makes you aware of your reactions to any limiting beliefs you may have about yourself. Only by bringing these beliefs to the surface can you recognize them for what they are—limitations that you have set yourself, based on the opinion or behaviour of someone you trusted.

Exercise 2

To identify your triggers, take each of your fears, habits, etc, then ask yourself what kind of person would behave or allow themselves to be treated in this way. Keep asking the question until you end up with one of the triggers.

Examples:

I think (believe) I'm unattractive.
Q: What kind of person would think they are unattractive? → A: Someone who is unlovable.

I need my partner to help me make decisions.
Q: What kind of person would need their partner to help them make decisions? → A: Someone who is unsure of themselves.

Q: What kind of person would be unsure of themselves? → A: Someone who is powerless/weak.

Using the information gathered in Exercise 1, identify your main triggers on the following chart.

What kind of person would…?	*Trigger:*

Once you have identified your main triggers, you have a powerful tool with which to begin interrupting your cycles. Whenever your triggers are activated, and you feel powerless, for example, your body usually reacts on a physical level. This bodily reaction is very important in helping you break out of your cycle. It represents the subconscious memory of what led you to believe that you were powerless, worthless, unlovable, etc, in the first place. The body's reaction (e.g. tension in stomach or shoulders/neck) is the first warning sign that you are about to go into your reactive cycle—the way you instinctively react when your trigger is activated.

Are you free of charge? The following exercise enables you to progressively defuse the charge behind your triggers and break out of your usual reactive cycle. If you are not operating free of charge, you are probably paying the price.

Exercise 3

1. STOP *as soon as you feel your body tense. Your stomach may clench, your shoulders may tighten or your breathing may constrict. Whatever the physical symptom, it is your body's 'red flag', indicating that your trigger has just been activated. Acknowledging that this physical symptom is directly wired to your emotional reaction is the first step towards breaking your cycle.*

2. IDENTIFY *the trigger (powerless, unimportant, etc) that has just been activated and take a few deep breaths to give your body time to process your awareness of what is going on.*

3. REMIND *yourself that you are just about to go into your usual reactive behaviour. You may typically flare up in anger or you might bite back your words. You might freeze on the spot or run from the room. Identify what your usual reaction would be and see how it has been running your life. Remind yourself also that your reaction was learned and has nothing to do with your true value.*

4. ACKNOWLEDGE *that your reaction is perpetuating your cycle and that you are only being triggered so that you can respond differently and heal this old wound. Bear in mind that it keeps happening only because you keep reacting (and thereby reinforcing your cycle). The activation of your trigger is your best opportunity to break the cycle and create positive change.*

5. CHOOSE *to respond differently, knowing that your response has a direct impact on how others respond to you. If you would normally clam up, then say one or two words, no matter how shakily. If you would normally run from the room, try to stand your ground for a few moments, knowing that changing your pattern is the only way to break your cycle. Imagine how good it will feel afterwards to have said or done what you wanted, despite the anxiety you felt inside.*

6. CONGRATULATE *yourself for every word or action that you manage to positively transform. Even if you have not said all that you wanted to say, acknowledge yourself for having started the process, and commit to building on your new approach each time your trigger is activated. It is very important to acknowledge yourself for whatever positive steps you take, no matter how seemingly insigificant.*

Although the tension or anxiety in your body will not disappear overnight, it will lessen as you practise this process of slowly transforming your response to the outside world. Forcing yourself to change in this way may seem contrived or stilted at first, but it soon becomes a habit that you are comfortable with. It is also a process that will inspire and empower you, increasing your self-esteem and self-acceptance. Reacting with anger or defensiveness always implies guilt, even if you have done nothing wrong. By avoiding such reactions, you will be projecting an image of confidence, and you will begin to feel good about yourself.

How one powerful trigger came into Laura's life—and stayed

The following story illustrates how even one short conversation can create a trigger of monumental significance.

Laura was nine when it happened. Born to two loving and conscientious parents, she had a great deal of love and affection, all that she needed materially, and just the right amount of gentle discipline to teach her healthy respect. She was sitting on her father's lap one evening after he had read her a story. The story was about a young man who saved his loved one from drowning, and it prompted Laura to ask her father the following question: "Who would you save first, Daddy, if Mummy and I were both drowning at the same time?" Her father, priding himself in always being honest with his daughter, thought for a long moment before replying. "I'd save your mother first," he said. "Then I'd save you."

Laura's life did not deteriorate immediately following that conversation, but her intimate relationships in later years were haunted and driven by the subconscious memory of what her father had said—with all its powerful implications. The conclusion she came to about herself was that she was unimportant. This belief brought with it the firm conviction that she was not worthy of being fully loved by a man. As a result, she consistently sabotaged her relationships, subconsciously creating 'legitimate' reasons for abandoning her partner before he could fulfill her fears and abandon her.

Avoiding potential pitfalls

- ***Don't let yourself be distracted by circumstances or someone else's issues.*** *Circumstances are merely the external manifestation of what is happening, or still missing, inside you.*
- ***Don't seek approval for any changes you make or for working on your issues.*** *Approval must come from within yourself, and needing it from others will keep you stuck in your cycle.*
- ***Don't underestimate your progress, however slight it may seem.*** *Be sure to acknowledge yourself for every little positive change that you make, as doing this will further enhance your self-worth.*

Chapter 4

Filling in the missing pieces

To the degree that something is missing in you, it will be missing in your life.

Your reactive, self-defeating cycles are based on your 'missing pieces'. These are the emotional qualities that you needed as a child but did not get—such as acceptance, validation, affection, support, respect, encouragement, etc.

The process of filling in your missing pieces is the key to getting what you want out of life. You may make many other positive changes, but if you do not fill in your missing pieces you will continue to create cycles or dynamics that prevent you from finding fulfillment.

To start the process, you must first determine exactly what is missing. (See Exercise 4, page 49, on how to identify your particular missing pieces.) Bear in mind the ingredients (such as acceptance, respect, trust, understanding and support) that would be required for your relationships to be harmonious, intimate and mutually supportive. If you are missing these important ingredients within yourself, imagine what kind of relationships you would create as a result. Identifying what is missing in you will give you a clear idea of why your relationships are the way they are.

When you examine this list to see which of those things you do not give yourself in your life, and which you do not give to others, you will have identified your 'missing pieces'. And, to the extent that they are missing in you, they are undoubtedly missing in your life. These are aspects of love that you may have lacked as a child and, therefore, never learned how to give to yourself or others. Because these qualities were missing in your early development, they are outside your frame of reference and your comfort zone as an adult. They are also subconsciously beyond your ability to integrate, since you were taught, by implication, that you did not deserve them.

When we are missing key emotional qualities in our lives, we can end up creating a cycle of neediness whereby we are constantly trying to get those missing elements from our partner (see 'The neediness cycle' on page 60). This cycle of need, expectation and disappointment can eventually lead to resignation, exhaustion, defeat and cynicism. The cycle only needs to repeat itself once or twice for individuals to become convinced that they are hapless 'victims', completely at the mercy of this 'outside force'.

The four most fundamental 'missing pieces' are **acceptance, trust, authenticity and intimacy**. These aspects of love are essential to our personal fulfillment and growth. When consecutively filled in, these missing pieces also constitute a process that culminates in deep inner contentment and joy.

Acceptance of ourselves and of others is fundamental to our well-being. But it is not about blindly accepting whatever comes our way; it is a state of mind in which we practise loving and accepting ourselves and others in positive, healthy ways, respecting them but not necessarily associating with them if they do not nurture or support us.

In learning and practising acceptance, we learn trust; in learning and practising trust, we come to an understanding of authenticity; and in practising authenticity, we come, finally, to the expression and experience of true intimacy. All four elements are necessary for self-understanding and fulfillment.

In restoring what has been missing in our lives, and therefore mastering those same qualities, we reach the deepest possible level of intimacy with ourselves and others. It is the need to look at what is not working in our lives that leads us to the exploration and discovery of our uniqueness. This uniqueness is our personal gift to the world. The degree to which elements such as acceptance and trust are lacking, then, is the degree to which we are separated or disconnected from our unique life's purpose.

Identifying what is missing in you will give you a clear idea of why your relationships are the way they are.

Missing piece 1:

Acceptance

Our quest for acceptance is the single greatest human motivator, compelling us to grow, reach out, and fulfill our potential. However, it is also the main cause of dysfunctional relationships. In childhood, as soon as we can understand the concept of 'no' (and sometimes even sooner), we learn that we are not totally and unconditionally acceptable. If we are born to critical parents (who may not have been considered acceptable by their parents or peers), we quickly learn that we have to distort ourselves in order to meet our parents' idea of acceptability. Because our survival is in the hands of our parents, we have no choice but to conform and to fit their image of what we should be. Thus we learn the arts of deception and dissimulation. Pretending to be something we are not, we learn how to suppress and deny our feelings. And, throughout it all, we learn fear.

As adults, this fear keeps us in a constant state of wariness, always on the look-out for criticism or rejection that will rub salt in the old wound of unacceptability. What we learn about our apparent failings, as children, can translate into a lifetime of dissatisfaction. We may devise a multitude of strategies designed to generate acceptance from others; but, because this acceptance is missing on the inside, we rarely attract it on the outside. We may crave it, but we learned that we did not deserve it. This deep-seated need brings with it the fear that we will never get it. We then build an association between need and fear, so that what we most want in life becomes what we are also most afraid of having.

Ironically, then, when a glimmer of acceptability does come our way, we often reject it, believing ourselves to be unworthy of it. Or we may run from it, because it is so unfamiliar that it makes us uncomfortable.

As we grow up, we enhance any learned patterns or beliefs of unacceptability. We literally take up where our parents left off, criticizing ourselves in our minds, berating ourselves when we make a mistake, and often abandoning dreams because we so deeply believe we are not good enough to realize them. If we treated our friends the way we often treat ourselves in our minds, we would lead a very alienated existence.

The key to restoring acceptance in our lives is to fill in the missing piece on the inside. Acceptance is an internal phenomenon that begins with the self. It is not about putting up with, or making right, everything that is happening in our life; it is about reconciling with ourselves and making ourselves acceptable, in our own mind, to the rest of the world. This can be done by using the self as a parameter for determining what is good for us. For example, we may be in the habit of compromising our needs and over-extending ourselves by doing things for other people. This tendency conveys low self-worth; it establishes expectations from others who believe that we will continue to meet their needs, and that our needs are less important than theirs. We have told them so, through our behaviour towards them. When the way we relate to others is based on healthy self-acceptance (i.e., putting ourselves first in a healthy, holistic way, and saying "no" to helping others when our own needs have not been met), then that level of acceptance will start to be reflected back to us by others. We will have increased our sense of value—both to ourselves and to them. By being less willing to give them so much of ourselves, we make ourselves a more highly valued 'commodity'. 'More is less' in the sense that giving too much to others suggests that we are inferior to them. It implies that we need to give 150% to make up everyone else's 100%. Placing a higher value on ourselves also commands greater respect and makes us less vulnerable to the expectations of needy individuals.

Generating genuine self-acceptance means practising acceptance in every area of our life where it is lacking or deficient. It means catching ourselves when we put ourselves down and, instead, reassuring and acknowledging ourselves; it means doing very practical things to demonstrate our self-acceptance; and it means practising acceptance with the very people in our life who seem least deserving of it.

However, it is not a matter of practising acceptance merely so that we receive it back. We need to practise it because we never learned it. We need to practise it until it becomes a natural reflex, integrated into our personality and belief system. And we need to practise it with others so that we teach them how we would like to be treated. Those close to us usually have the same missing pieces, and therefore cannot give us what they never learned themselves. They are in our life to show us what is missing, and they provide us with the opportunity to be powerful catalysts for them and us. This is especially

When the way you relate to others is based on healthy self-acceptance, then that level of acceptance will start to be reflected back to you by others.

true of family—the original source of our missing pieces. Parents who themselves lacked acceptance would be incapable of giving it to their children, no matter how much the children needed it.

Self-acceptance means allowing ourselves to be unique in our thoughts, self-expression, style, creativity, behaviour and choices, regardless of what others might think.

Simply affirming our self-worth is not always enough to restore the missing pieces in our lives. Sometimes this can even increase the conflict between what we actually think, say and do every day, and how we would ideally like to think or behave. However, this is extremely powerful when combined with positive action. When we begin to relate differently to ourselves and others, we begin to break the cycle of self-criticism and replace it with one of acceptance. It is through conscious interaction with others that we change our subconscious beliefs and our automatic reactions. We also change our electromagnetic field and the messages that we transmit to the outside world.

Practical ways in which we can start to show ourselves acceptance include acknowledging and supporting ourselves in any decision that we make; accepting compliments graciously; putting ourselves first in a way that enhances our health and well-being; rewarding ourselves for things we have done well, and comforting ourselves for those we feel we have not; and dressing or presenting ourselves in a way that reflects our personal taste and flair. Self-acceptance means allowing ourselves to be unique in our thoughts, self-expression, style, creativity, behaviour and choices, regardless of what others might think.

Demonstrating acceptance of others involves focusing on the positive in them, rather than criticizing their faults; acknowledging and supporting them in all that they do; complimenting them on their good qualities; taking an interest in their opinions and uniqueness; and accepting their beliefs and choices even if we do not necessarily agree with them. Accepting others also means not trying to change them, fix them, or make them into what we think they should be.

However, acceptance of self and others is not about being a doormat or allowing oneself to be treated in abusive or manipulative ways. The criteria for acceptance are based on what is beneficial and constructive for our health and well-being. Once we understand the dynamic of attraction and reaction, we realize that we can only bring about change in others by changing ourselves. This dynamic applies as much to personal relationships as it does to environmental and political issues. Once mastered at the personal level and practised by more and more individuals, it has the power to create change at the global level.

When faced with the challenges of practising unconditional acceptance, it is important to remember that those who are triggering this issue in us are there because we 'put them there'. In other words, when acceptance is a 'missing piece' in us, we literally attract individuals and circumstances that reflect back to us that missing piece. People tend to treat us the way we subconsciously believe we deserve to be treated. The universe will always support that belief, and the choices that we make as a result.

As we change the way we treat ourselves—on the inside and in the way we dress, walk, talk and act—others will begin to respond accordingly. As we raise our self-esteem, we generate greater acceptance on the outside. We begin to see magic happen. And we will begin to realize a fundamental truth: the main purpose of our relationships with others is to learn who we are, by seeing reflected back to us whatever we subconsciously believe ourselves to be.

Instead of seeing ourselves as the victim of others' words or actions, we will begin to see ourselves as the enabler and perpetuator of the whole process. In other words, only because we are the way we are, can others be the way they are. It is like a game requiring two players.

As we raise our self-esteem, we generate greater acceptance on the outside. We begin to see magic happen.

Once one refuses to play, the game ends. Once we decide to act, think and practise what we intend ourselves to be, others can no longer continue to treat us as they did before.

To more effectively create this shift, we must remember to be proactive in your feelings and focus, rather than being reactive to what seemingly 'comes at us'. (See Chapter 11: 'Focus and projection'.)

There is nothing more gratifying than unconditional acceptance, and nothing curdles our insides more than its opposite—criticism, disapproval and rejection.

The pursuit of self-acceptance is a lifelong preoccupation, with many highs and lows along the way. The closest most people come to experiencing unconditional acceptance is in the early stages of an intimate relationship. At the beginning of the relationship, there is often the heady euphoria of 'falling in love'—the direct result of feeling totally accepted by someone whom we, initially, find more than acceptable. However, once the early romance fades, issues of commitment and intimacy begin to trigger old insecurities, and our acceptance becomes conditional. We begin to see the other's 'faults' (which have actually been there all along), and to build a case for their unacceptability. This is usually the result of our own unacceptability coming to the surface. But, ironically, it gets projected onto our partner so that we can avoid acknowledging our own perceived shortcomings.

Both the bliss of falling in love and the pain of rejection are caused by our habitual lack of self-acceptance. We do not heal the imbalance by finding the 'right' man or woman, but by replacing the missing piece of acceptance within us, which then enables us to attract a similarly accepting partner. Practising and restoring acceptance can be done in almost any relationship, provided that it is within a framework of conscious responsibility for having attracted what we most needed to learn.

There is nothing more gratifying than unconditional acceptance, and nothing curdles our insides more than its opposite—criticism, disapproval and rejection.

Restoring acceptance means:

- *acknowledging that you are acceptable just the way you are, with all the tools you need in order to create what you want;*
- *treating everyone else as equally acceptable, without judgement, even if you do not necessarily like them;*
- *reminding yourself that you attract certain situations and relationships in order to discover who you are and what you can become;*
- *knowing that you are never the victim of others but a powerful being who attracts the very people who trigger your issues and present you with the opportunity to resolve them;*
- *remembering that, by meeting other people's expectations, you are teaching those people how to treat you;*
- *treating yourself with respect, compassion and acceptance, aware that, in doing so, you attract people who do likewise;*
- *catching yourself when you find fault with others—a reminder that you still have not fully accepted yourself;*
- *validating others' contributions, opinions and uniqueness as you do your own; and*
- *expressing what you feel and asking for what you want, out of respect and love for yourself.*

When you have practised, lived and integrated acceptance to the point where it is no longer an issue in your life, you will already have embarked upon the road to trust—the second of the four major missing pieces.

Missing piece 2:

Trust

Contrary to popular opinion, trust is not necessarily something that is earned. It may seem as if others must prove their trustworthiness to us, through their actions or words, but trust is actually born more of a conscious decision than an external dynamic.

As with acceptance, or any other missing piece, the absence of trustworthy people in our lives is a reflection of a lack of inner trust. At some early stage in our development, we were let down by someone who mattered. At a time in our lives when we were open and vulnerable, unconditionally trusting the world, someone violated that trust. From that moment forth, we decided never to trust again. We did not revert to unconditional trusting after that painful experience (although we might have claimed to), but carried our wariness with us, in readiness for the next violation. But deciding not to trust creates a vacuum within us, attracting situations, people and relationships that constantly trigger and reinforce our belief in others' untrustworthiness.

A child's limited frame of reference creates absolutes. At the age of three or four, when our conscious world is made up almost exclusively of our parents, we automatically assume that what our father or mother does to us is representative of the world at large. What we learn in this formative stage of childhood becomes the filter through which we view and interpret all others later in life.

When we learn mistrust, and trust becomes a missing piece, we begin to live a more reactive life. Mistrust cramps our style. Rather than being spontaneous in our words or actions, we become guarded, cautious and inhibited. Where we might otherwise have plunged whole-heartedly into some activity, we may instead try to determine people's level of trustworthiness, either anticipating a let-down, or merely experiencing an uneasiness that prevents us from total involvement. We learn not to trust, and so our world becomes filled with those who show us that trust is missing.

As with acceptance, the key to restoring trust is to practise it, inside and out. This means practising conscious decision-making. Almost everything we do in life is about making choices or decisions. Do we walk to the bank or take the car? Should we phone our mother-in-law and apologize or wait for her to do it? Should we call that new guy/girl at the office or play hard to get? We are constantly challenged by the necessity of making choices. But making choices that support and benefit us must always be based on trust. Without that inner sounding board, we have no way of feeling good about our choices, and instead agonize over what we might or should have done or said.

Those who have learned mistrust early in life may also have trouble knowing what or who they want to be. These are often individuals whose parents had rigid ideas about what was and was not the 'right' thing to do. When children grow up in this environment of limited possibilities, they often lose the ability to make choices and trust their inner voice. By the time they reach their mid-teens, such individuals no longer trust themselves. By the time they are in their mid-30s, they no longer trust anyone else either.

But re-creating the bigger picture of career and purpose in life begins with practising small-scale, everyday decision-making. Not only are individuals re-learning inner trust, but they are also reconnecting with that buried passionate part of themselves that would naturally propel them towards what they most want to do in life.

Practising self-trust involves reconnecting with the physical body. When we are in a state of uneasiness, due to mistrust, we experience a corresponding physical sensation. For some, it is a tension in the shoulders or upper back; for others, it is a knot in the stomach. Whatever the sensation, this is the 'red flag' that alerts us to the fact that we are doing or saying something that probably does not serve us. It is our radar system warning us to do something about it. In such cases, it is not a matter of forcing ourselves to trust the person involved, but rather to trust our body's natural instincts in determining whether we should do what is being asked of us. This means being able to tell the difference between long-standing mistrust of self and people in general, and appropriate non-involvement. It also means being able to distinguish between intuition and fear. Getting to that point of inner certainty requires practice.

When mistrust has been a constant companion, however, we often learn to ignore or tolerate the physical discomfort (our radar system) that goes with it. We start to switch off the bodily reactions and focus on merely surviving a threatening situation. But this physical reaction is the key to rebuilding trust—both of ourselves and of others.

Whenever we are called upon to make a choice or decision, we must immediately tune in to that part of our body

Mistrust cramps our style.

Our decisions are often made on the basis of what others want.

Our parents teach us this one early.

that sends us warning signals. Many of us can identify numerous occasions when we knew we should have said "no" to someone, but ended up saying "yes", for whatever reason. Our 'wrong' decision gnaws at us inside, making us uneasy or resentful about what we have committed to doing. Rarely, however, do we backtrack and change our answer to a 'no'. And rarely do we remember, the next time, that we would be better served by saying "no" instead of "yes". Mistrust of ourselves often means that we give in too readily to the demands and expectations of others, at the expense of our own needs or wants. In the absence of self-trust, then, our decisions are often made on the basis of what others want.

Our parents teach us this one early. They naturally expect us to do what they consider to be best. We often translate this into the general expectations of others, compromising our needs and wishes in favour of theirs. And so we can end up deferring to others, rather than trusting our own judgement. This can make *us* untrustworthy, in that we may sometimes side with whoever may be placing the greatest pressure on us to give them what they want. And so the cycle of mistrust continues.

To begin developing self-trust, we can use the body as our guide. When we experience tension or uneasiness in our shoulders, chest, solar plexus or elsewhere, it is usually a sign that we are somehow not respecting or honouring ourselves. To break this cycle, we must stop whatever we are doing in the moment. Whether we are in the middle of a conversation, or about to call someone, we need to start listening to, and respecting, that inner feeling. We need to start 'flexing' that part of us as if it were an unused muscle.

As we focus on our body's 'red flag', the sensation either intensifies or decreases, depending on how much we respect it. It always tells us what is best for us, once we learn how to correctly interpret it.

We must also use our minds to rebuild trust. This means constantly asking ourselves if what we are doing is what we want. It means discriminating between obligation and desire. Do you really want to go to that movie, or do you only think you should, because you said you would? Are you really interested in attending that workshop, or are you only going because it is free and everyone else in your group raves about it? These may seem like insignificant choices in the bigger picture of career, relationship or home, but they form the essential foundation for what is trying to evolve within us. For each time that we deny what we want, in favour of what we think we should be doing, we are not only reinforcing our inner mistrust, but we are not allowing our innate guidance mechanism to lead us where we ultimately want to go.

For example, if we respect the fact that we are not interested in attending a particular event, but instead respond to the urge to visit the local café, we might well encounter someone or gain some valuable insight that has a significant impact on our life. Such seemingly fortuitous 'twists of fate' have often led to outcomes as significant as a new career, the beginning of a relationship, or a move to another country. (See 'Trusting your instincts' overleaf.)

We should never underestimate the power of our inclinations. But unearthing them requires patience and commitment to trust. This means not just trusting yourself to do something right, but also trusting that, as long as you are following your heart, everything will be taken care of.

Only by consciously making a habit of doing and saying what we want or feel, can we start to rebuild our trust of self and others.

Another way to do this would be to set aside a day exclusively for yourself. This is a day in which you only do what you feel like doing, no matter how indulgent. It is a day for making choices on a whim—saying "no" to babysitting for a friend because you want to spend

We should never underestimate the power of our inclinations. But unearthing them requires patience and commitment to trust. This means not just trusting yourself to do something right, but also trusting that, as long as you are following your heart, everything will be taken care of.

Trusting your instincts

Many key turning points in my life have been the result of my trusting an intuitive impulse. Meeting the man I would ultimately marry was one of the most significant of these.

I had been living in Vancouver, Canada for nine years, having moved there from Switzerland in the early 1990s. However, in 2001, I felt a strong urge to return to Switzerland. This surprised me as I had left for good reasons and never expect to return. I resisted the urge for some time, unable to figure out why I should go back. I had no significant connections there, I had lost touch with many of my former friends and I knew that the Swiss lifestyle did not really suit me; although extremely beautiful, Switzerland somehow lacked heart and soul.

But the urge remained strong, and several aspects of my life in Vancouver seemed to be drawing to a natural close. I finally decided to go to Switzerland for a few months, if only to satisfy the strange yearning that I felt. I tapped into some of my former work-related contacts in Geneva and obtained a short-term contract as an editor.

When I arrived in Switzerland, I felt huge resistance to being there. I knew that my work as an editor was not going to bring me any great personal fulfillment and I already missed my close friends in Canada. Six months later, I was still wracked with doubt over my decision to come back. Had I made a mistake? Why was I back here when Vancouver was so obviously a much better 'fit' for me? I was sitting in my rental car one afternoon, when I decided to ask for a sign from the universe—an unequivocal sign that would tell me clearly what to do. I turned on the radio and a song was playing: "Should I stay or should I go? …If I stay there will be trouble. If I leave it will be double." *Well, it could hardly have been clearer. I had my answer. Even so, I found myself asking the same questions again a few months later. I was sitting at the lakeside when I asked for another sign.* Should I stay or should I leave, *I wanted to know. I sat in silence for a few moments and then heard voices nearby. A woman was playing with her dog. It started tugging at its leash and the woman called out, "Stay! Stay!" I had to smile. This message was as graphic as the last one.*

Two months later, I met a very special man and I knew why I had been prompted to return to Switzerland. We were married a year later and returned to Canada shortly afterwards.

The reasons for our intuitive urges are not always clear, at first, but if we can trust that these urges are there for a reason and can go along with them, despite our fears, they can take us to places we never dreamed of.

two hours soaking in the bathtub, with a mountain of bubbles and soft candlelight. It means being childlike in terms of choosing to do—or not do—something, simply because you do or do not feel like it. We have all seen children stubbornly refusing to do what they are told. A child adamantly sticks to what feels right, often despite heavy parental pressure. As adults, we are often obsessed with needing to know why someone did something. When we place this same expectation on children, they usually defeat us with the unarguable assertion that they just 'felt like it'. As adults, we need to do more of that.

Having a sacred day for self helps you to switch off the mind and focus on the heart. There must be no set timetable and your wristwatch should not be worn that day. At first, having a totally open, unscheduled day ahead of you may seem daunting; few of us are comfortable with large chunks of time doing nothing. The challenge here is to keep tuning in to what feels right in the moment—and not planning ahead.

As you practise this, you start to be guided by your deeper inclinations, and you start to trust those feelings. For instance, you may suddenly think of an old friend you haven't talked to for months and feel compelled to call her. There is usually a good reason. Trust it. Even if nothing seemingly significant results, you will be practising acting on your instincts, and reinforcing trust in the process.

Your sacred day is just that—sacred. Therefore, practise keeping it free for yourself, no matter how many friends or relatives need you to do something for them. We all love to feel needed, but not giving in to that need is yet another dimension of trust. By honouring yourself and keeping this day free, you are trusting that your friends value you for who you are, rather than for what you can do for them. And if, in the process, your friends actually reject you for 'letting them down', then this exercise will have been doubly beneficial; not only will you have made a significant step forward in reinforcing your self-trust, but you will also have made a distinction between true friends and 'users'.

If your 'friends' do reject you once you start taking care of yourself in this way, it is not cause for greater mistrust. Instead, it is your heart guiding you towards healthier, more rewarding friendships. Unless you clear out the old patterns, there is no room for the new. Trust that, too.

Trusting means going with your inner feelings, without knowing where they will lead you. Acting only in possession of all the facts and possible outcomes is not trust; it is merely logic, which has nothing to do with inspiration, instinct and dreams of the heart.

Often, if we are wracked by indecision (mistrust of self), the only solution is to make a choice, even if we are not sure it is the most appropriate one. In this way, we can gauge the 'rightness' or 'wrongness' of it and can then more clearly see if that was what we originally wanted. Few everyday choices are so momentous that they cannot be reversed. And their reversal, in itself, can be an important part of the process of building self-trust.

Often, too, the answer is in the question. If, for example, you are unsure whether you should stay in your current job or do something completely different, you might want to ask yourself why you are even thinking this way. Something inside is telling you that you are unhappy with your current position. Not being able to think of what you would prefer to do instead is not a reason to distrust your feeling. Only by deciding to trust that feeling do you give it room to expand and create an opening for new possibilities. Trusting means going with your inner feelings, without knowing where they will lead you. Acting only in possession of all the facts and possible outcomes is not trust; it is merely logic, which has nothing to do with inspiration, instinct and dreams of the heart.

Practising trust of others is an extension of self-trust. If you trust yourself and practise following your instincts, you can also begin to trust that you will choose trustworthy friends, partners and employers. Remember: any absence of trust in your life is a reflection of your own lack of trust in yourself. Often we are convinced that we *do* trust ourselves, only to realize later that we felt one thing but did another. This is why the practical applications of trusting are so important. It is not enough to affirm that you trust yourself. You must live accordingly. You must live a self-trusting life.

Restoring trust means acknowledging that:

- *you are always in the right place, faced with the perfect opportunities for growth;*
- *if you follow your heart and feelings, you will get what you need and want;*
- *whatever is truly best for you is usually also best for everyone else concerned—even if they do not always see it that way;*
- *by following your heart and doing what you want, you are breaking free of old self-defeating cycles—and making room for better things;*
- *whoever is in your life (no matter how threatening or unpleasant) is only there because you attracted them to you so that you could discover and fill in what was missing within;*
- *your gut feeling will always keep you on track;*
- *being yourself is your greatest gift—to yourself and others; and*
- *through consciously filling in the missing pieces, you create the relationships, situations and circumstances that you want in your life.*

Once self-trust has become familiar and natural, readily expressed in your choices, friendships, conversations and behaviour, you are ready to embrace the third major missing piece: authenticity.

Missing piece 3:

Authenticity

Authenticity is the return to self—a process of rediscovery, based on trust and self-acceptance. Since the true self often goes underground at around the age of three, the search for one's authentic self must take place in the present moment.

Reclaiming our authenticity, then, requires presence of mind. We must be fully present and self-aware in order to be true to ourselves in our thoughts, actions, intentions and words.

Our essential qualities are always innate, no matter how deeply buried. However, bringing them back to the surface can be a painful and challenging process. Doing so involves practising total honesty with ourselves and others in every moment, regardless of old habits, expectations or resentments. This requires perpetual monitoring of our feelings, to ensure that our thoughts and actions are based on heartfelt sincerity. If there is an absence of sincerity in anything we do, there is an absence of authenticity. **If we are not behaving in accordance with our heart, we are not being authentically ourselves.**

In order to fully restore our authentic self, we may need to completely overhaul our life. This may involve changing the company we keep, the clothes we wear, the language we use, the job we do, or the relationships we have. But it is a gradual process of refinement—a journey unto itself—not to be undertaken lightly or with too much fervour or speed. The process itself must be heartfelt and genuine.

When assessing our life for its authenticity, the key question to ask ourselves is whether or not a particular person, thing or relationship makes us feel good on all levels—physical, emotional, mental and spiritual. If it does not serve us in these ways, it does not belong in our life. It may well have become part of our life because of obligation, habit, need or addiction, but it may be preventing us from living authentically.

Maintaining such habits, obligations or addictions means living a lie. It means settling for something other than what would make us happy. It means living out of fear, which is always based on what is missing, rather than on what should be. And it means making the rest of the world more important than ourselves. Such patterns stand in the way of truth by blocking or suppressing our expression of what would make us feel good on all levels. Anything less than authenticity is a compromise—the foundation of mediocrity. If we are happy with a mediocre life, we do not need authenticity. But if our life lacks lustre, if our heart feels flat and weary, and if our relationships do not bring us unmitigated joy, then authenticity is probably the missing ingredient.

Compromise—and therefore mediocrity—is the result of the choices we make. The path to authenticity, then, is one of consciously choosing, based on whether something or someone nourishes us on all levels.

Creating authenticity means choosing to:

- ***maintain friendships only with those who love and support you;***
- ***pursue a line of work that has meaning for you;***
- ***speak and act with honesty and integrity, regardless of the expected outcome;***
- ***be honest and sincere with yourself regarding your motivations;***
- ***make decisions out of choice, rather than fear;***
- ***spontaneously show and express your emotions in the moment (provided that doing so does not harm anyone);***
- ***speak your mind, based on your own beliefs and values rather than trying to impress others with what you think they want to hear;***
- ***be as you are in that moment, without pretending to be something you are not; and***
- ***share the gift of your uniqueness.***

When you are comfortable with, and experienced in, the art of living authentically, then you are ready for the ultimate challenge: true intimacy.

Missing piece 4:

Intimacy

While acceptance may well be what everyone ideally wants in life, its ultimate expression—intimacy—has the power to terrify even the most self-assured. Intimacy is far more than sexual closeness. It is authenticity coupled with spirituality. It is the naked exposure of one's deepest feelings—the vulnerability of openness in expressing one's doubts, fears, beliefs, grief, affection, love, passion, humour and spirituality. It is the full expression of self, without façade, control, dissimulation, contrivance, manipulation or inhibition. Intimacy is about the simplicity of *being*, rather than the complexity of *doing*. It has less to do with who and what you are, than with *how* you are.

Such honesty does not come easily to most people. We have been taught to hide certain parts of ourselves, in order to be socially or otherwise acceptable; we have learned that it is not safe to be vulnerable emotionally, as others can hurt us; and, without acceptance and trust, we do not feel safe enough to be ourselves, for fear of rejection.

When confronted with a relationship and the prospect of intimacy, we can often devise a multitude of strategies for avoiding or deflecting that closeness. We can use the busyness of our lives as a very 'justifiable' distraction from going deeper with our partner. An active mind and body cancel out the possibility of a still heart and spirit—those parts of us that generate true intimacy.

Humour, sarcasm or flippancy are other methods used to deflect closeness. Laughter is an essential ingredient in life, building rapport and a sense of ease between people. However, when used as a defence mechanism, it can also act as a subtle, if unconscious, rebuff.

Starting an argument by finding fault with one's partner is another strategy guaranteed to distance anyone who gets too close. But whatever strategy is used, it is almost always applied unconsciously. Such defence mechanisms, developed in reaction to an early lack of affection or love, automatically kick in whenever intimacy seems imminent. When love and affection are unfamiliar, they are threatening, since the ability to deal with them healthily was never learned. It is said that familiarity breeds contempt; while that may not be altogether true, it is certainly accurate to say that unfamiliarity breeds fear.

The first step towards generating greater intimacy, then, is to identify one's strategy for keeping it at bay. What do you automatically do or say when you become uncomfortably close to someone? How do you hide your nervousness or fear? Do you choose relationships in which your partner is geographically, emotionally or otherwise unavailable? If you find yourself bemoaning the fact that your partner is too busy for you, does not give you enough affection, or is hard to talk to about intimate matters, then remember that you chose this particular dynamic, as embodied by this particular partner. And, this being the case, he/she is a reflection of your issues (your missing pieces). What kind of person would choose a partner who is distant or unavailable? The objective answer would be: someone who does not think he/she deserves closeness (i.e., love) and the intimacy that comes with having 100% of a person. If some part of your partner is being withheld, look at what parts of yourself you are holding back.

This is perhaps the hardest missing piece to replace because we can usually find very sound arguments to support our theory that it is our partner who is distant, not us. When we attract a distant or emotionally unavailable partner, we will probably spend a great deal of energy trying to reach that person. We may repeatedly ask for more affection, attention or closeness, and may even arrange romantic candlelight dinners in the hope of generating some intimacy. The fallacy in this line of reasoning, however, is that we have subconsciously chosen a partner who can never provide that intimacy, because intimacy is a quality that we are missing inside; as a result, we can safely claim to be open to intimacy and to do our utmost to bring it into the relationship.

If we were, somehow, to attract someone who was readily available in every way, we would probably find the tables rapidly turned. The dynamic of the relationship would switch from unavailability/pursuit, to availability/retreat. The individual who was so used to his/her partner being unavailable would have no frame of reference with which to deal with the potential intimacy that comes from total availability.

Recognizing—and admitting to—these complex strategies is the hard part. However, once we catch ourselves at our own game, we are in a powerful position to change things for the better. Once we acknowledge that our partner's issues are the perfect foil to ours, we begin to understand how we have set ourselves up for a never-ending cycle of personal defeat and deprivation. But we also realize that we have the power to break free of this cycle for good.

Even though we may become more comfortable with the four major missing pieces, we rarely, if ever, reach the stage where we are absolutely and unconditionally accepting, trusting, authentic or intimate. However, by continuing to practise these qualities, we can experience them more deeply, while perpetuating an increasingly positive cycle that brings ever-greater rewards.

Creating intimacy means:

- ***being open and honest from the very core of your being;***
- ***refusing to use distancing tactics such as humour or criticism to keep your partner at bay;***
- ***practising acceptance, trust and authenticity;***
- ***creating opportunities for physical, emotional and spiritual closeness;***
- ***allowing your innate femininity or masculinity to blossom (for example, for a woman to dress in a feminine way, rather than hiding her sexuality beneath masculine clothing);***
- ***allowing your deepest feelings to surface, no matter how scary it may be to share them with another;***
- ***surrendering to the love and passion that are trying to be expressed between you and your partner;***
- ***removing all obstacles to closeness, whether they are geographical distance, other commitments, fears or self-doubts;***
- ***dropping your façades or any attempts to appear to be other than who you are;***
- ***learning to be comfortable with joy and passion, as well as grief, no matter how unfamiliar they may feel at first;***
- ***loving yourself enough to allow someone you love to love you;***
- ***focusing on your similarities rather than your differences;***
- ***recognizing and respecting your partner's sensitivity; and***
- ***finding ways to reach and love your partner through your throughts, words and actions.***

Other missing pieces

Although **acceptance, trust, authenticity** and **intimacy** are the four most significant missing pieces in most individuals, there may be others that contribute to your particular cycle (see Exercise 4).

If, for example, good communication is another of your missing pieces, there are several ways to practise filling it in for yourself. Doing so would mean finding ways to reconnect with your feelings. With long-standing disconnectedness, the most common feeling is fear, which blocks you from feeling what is underneath. Communicating with yourself, and working on some of the other likely missing pieces (such as support and encouragement), can help you to reconnect with yourself.

Only by communicating honestly and openly with others can we truly discover who we are. When we communicate in this way, we transmit messages about our true selves. How we relate to the resulting exchanges determines the extent and nature of our growth.

Exercise 4

1. Make a list of all the things you need and would like to have (at an emotional level) from your ideal partner. In addition to the four major missing pieces listed above, your list may include, for example, respect, encouragement, support, good communication, thoughtfulness and validation.

2. Examine this list to see which of these things you do not get from your partner and do not give yourself. (This exercise can be done from either standpoint—looking at what your partner is not giving you, or looking at what you are not giving yourself or your partner. Either way, the elements that you identify will be missing somewhere in your relationships.) If you are not currently in a relationship, think back to your last one and use that as your barometer. Usually, whatever you are not giving to your partner, you are not giving to yourself, either. For example, if you are in the habit of not communicating your thoughts or feelings to your partner, it is likely that you do not fully acknowledge them to yourself. This leads to a form of denial or 'disconnectedness', which means that part of you is unavailable to your partner. If this is one of your missing pieces, it is more than likely that you are (or have been) in a relationship that lacks any great depth or intimacy.

3. Look at the ways in which you do not give yourself or your partner those things on your 'wish list'. Once again, this is because they were never given to you, and so never learned by you. Their absence, however, creates a need for them, but that need must now be met by you, not your partner.

4. On a daily basis, practise giving yourself those missing pieces in very practical ways. Do not be deterred if you seem to be challenged with your issues even more than usual; once you decide to confront them, you will be presented with plenty of opportunities for dealing with them. Your conscious decision to move forward prompts the universe to come to your aid and to enable you to reclaim yourself as fast as possible. The more you practise filling in your missing pieces with those around you, the faster they will become a natural part of you.

For example, practising communication could mean joining a singing class or a sports club, so that you can begin to communicate in non-threatening ways. It may also be as simple as starting a journal to resurrect buried thoughts and feelings, and then sharing those revelations with someone close to you.

Remember, only by filling in the missing pieces within yourself can you begin to attract those same qualities in your outside world—in a partner, in your work, or in any area of your life where such qualities have been missing.

Unconditionally giving to others is a gift that we simultaneously give to ourselves.

However, this must be done unconditionally. It is not a matter of only practising with those you like or those who would seem likely to return the same quality to you. It is about expressing yourself to everyone in your life, including those very people who do not seem to

The power of positive reinforcement

Just as we learn to doubt ourselves in certain ways when parents or teachers pass on their missing pieces to us, so too can we learn to believe in ourselves when others believe in us. When I was ten years old, I was staying with some friends of my parents in Cork, in southern Ireland. Their children—Peter and David—were roughly the same ages as myself and my sister, Yvonne, and so we played together quite happily. I remember one rainy weekend when we were all cooped up in the house and had nothing to do. We were getting bored and cranky, when Peter's mother Deirdre had an idea. "Olga, why don't you cut Peter's hair," she said, much to my mother's horror.

"Deirdre, are you mad?" said my mother. "She's only ten. She has no idea how to cut hair. She will ruin it."

"It will grow again," said Deirdre, handing me a pair of scissors and a comb. "Go into Peter's bedroom and have a go."

And so I did. Of course, I completely massacred Peter's hair and my mother was fully vindicated. Peter, on the other hand, loved the spiky effect and has, as far as I can see, continued to favour funky hairdos to this day. The experience was hugely significant for me, and I have been cutting hair ever since, although now I am much more proficient at it and my husband, friends, former boyfriends and family (including my mother) have had many a haircut over the years. I never trained as a hairdresser, but the positive encouragement given to me when I was ten was all I needed to nurture what turned out to be a natural talent.

communicate well with you, respect you, or support you. This is particularly challenging because, when we have unmet needs, and old wounds as a result, we tend to want the rest of the world to make it up to us. We want others to pay, or to make the first move. We feel hard done by and do not see why we should be the ones to repair the damage. However, our resentment can often get in the way of our needs being met.

The important thing to remember is that our needs and painful experiences of the past are a reflection of what's missing in us—not in the world.

Unconditionally giving to others, then, is a gift that we simultaneously give to ourselves. We have to practise what we never learned so that it becomes a natural, integral part of us and a natural part of our world.

There are some important distinctions to make when filling in your missing pieces. Although you may attract a partner who shows you what you are missing because he or she has the same missing pieces, your partner will not necessarily fill in those missing pieces for him/herself, just because you have filled in yours. Your partner is there to trigger your growth in specific ways, and the purpose of your relationship may not extend beyond that. If your partner does choose to fill in those same pieces, your relationship may continue to grow and strengthen in love and intimacy. But, if that does not happen, you will almost certainly want a more balanced relationship, since your self-worth will have increased and you will be ready to go deeper with someone else. When that happens, it is vital that you say "no" to what is no longer working for you (i.e., perhaps the current relationship), with honesty and love, thus setting you and your partner free for the next stage of your respective journeys. You will then attract a new partner who already has those pieces that you have just filled in.

Avoiding potential pitfalls

- ***Don't expect your partner to change just because you do.*** *By filling in your missing pieces, you will automatically attract a better relationship—either with your current partner (if he or she chooses to grow with you) or with someone else, who will already have the pieces you have newly filled in for yourself.*
- ***Don't change for the sake of your partner.*** *If you do, you will be perpetuating some aspect of co-dependence. Change for your own sake and you will reap far greater rewards.*
- ***Beware of creating drama with your partner and distracting yourself from the real issues.*** *If your relationship is lacking passion, you may subconsciously create very emotional scenes, just so that you feel more alive. Instead, try to dig down to the underlying emotions that led to the lack of passion in the first place.*
- ***Don't try to make your partner pay for having hurt you.*** *Remember that he or she is there to show you what is missing in you. The desire for revenge reinforces your misconception that you were not powerful enough to have put him or her in your life so that you could grow. (If there is abuse, you need to make it clear that that is unacceptable and it may be wise to leave. If you continue to allow it, then there are other missing pieces—such as self-respect—that you will need to fill in, in order to find the strength to move on.)*

Part III

Exploring relationship dynamics; practical tools for living a life of healthy balance and conscious choice

Chapter 5

Living in the grey zone: where love lies in limbo

To fear love is to fear life, and those who fear life are already three parts dead.

—Bertrand Russell

Living in the grey zone is no fun at all, yet it is where many of us live, much of the time. This is where we are when we fail to fully embrace life, remaining, instead, on its fringes, feeling little, living little and loving even less. It is a place of limbo between life and death, between yes and no, and between passion and numbness. We get there as a result of a lack of trust and belief in ourselves and in our ability to make a difference.

Our feelings of defeat are usually born of repeated disappointments, based on an early, deeply-engrained belief in the futility of life. Unable to attain or even glimpse happiness, we give up on the possibility of ever finding it. This is often compounded by the struggle and hardships suffered by our parents, and their own resentments and disappointments carried down from generations before. As a result, our subconscious becomes imprinted with negative expectations.

When we lack belief in ourselves, the spark in our hearts gradually fades, leaving us with lives of mediocrity and unfulfilled dreams. Without this fire, which is our creative energy—our life force—illness may manifest, sexual energy may dwindle, and we may adopt a negative, defeatist outlook on life. We may even argue with those who try to convince us that life could be better.

Living in the grey zone is often the result of a fear of success. Ironically, it is this fear, combined with a strong desire to succeed, that propels us into the grey zone. It is the internal conflict, caused by these two opposing forces, that prevents us from being passionately engaged in life. It is like trying to drive a car when it is stuck in neutral. The engine is revving and there is plenty of fuel, but the entire mechanism has been thrown out of gear. This constant internal struggle transmits mixed messages to our subconscious and to the universe, our provider. The lack of forward movement in our lives leads us to conclude that we are powerless, and we eventually stop even looking for first gear, so exhausted are we from the effort.

There are several steps involved in exiting the grey zone. The first, and most important, is that of acknowledging that you are currently in it—that you are not fully in life and that life is not fully in you. Ask yourself in what areas of your life you feel flat, numb or unfulfilled. What aspects of your life are made up of mind-numbing routine, devoid of lightness and laughter? In what kinds of situations are you negative, depressed or defeated? Look at whatever arguments you come up with for not doing things. What excuses do you have for not doing what you might want to do? If you have been meaning to go to the gym, but do not go, ask yourself why not. If you have had the desire to learn to dance or sing, why haven't you? The answers are important, for they tell you what your pay-off is for staying in the grey zone. They are the stronghold keeping you from fully embracing life, and having life embrace you back. The answers might be something like, "I'm too busy", or "I have two left feet and would make a fool of myself trying to dance". The pay-off might therefore be that of staying in your comfort zone, even though, if you were entirely honest with yourself, you would realize that the grey zone is not comfortable at all.

Whatever your rationale, allow yourself to experience the feeling that goes with it. Then dig deeper to find out what is more important than these things. Ask yourself what exactly you are doing that is keeping you so busy. Are you engaging in things that bring you joy? If not, ask yourself why you allow yourself to be kept busy by these things. If it is purely for money, then ask yourself what you are doing with the money you are working so hard to earn. Will that bring you the good feelings you would have experienced by going dancing or doing an aerobics class?

You may well find that you come up with extremely good justifications for not doing the things that would bring you pleasure. But don't forget that it is precisely these arguments that got you into the grey zone in the first place. There is very little victory in winning your own argument with yourself. In reality, you end up losing a big part of you—the part that is unique, spontaneous and creative. Saying, "Yes" to the things that you have habitually been resisting will generate a powerful flow of energy into your life and your body. Saying "Yes", regardless of your resistance, will give the universe permission to support you.

You may find that you come up with seemingly justifiable reasons for not doing the things that would bring you pleasure.

Only by fully expressing suppressed grief can you break through the layers of numbness to find the rest of you—and probably the best of you.

Another important step involved in leaving the grey zone is the expression of any suppressed grief. Once you acknowledge that you have been living in this zone, you may feel that you have been wasting your life, treading water without going anywhere. This can often bring up a lot of sadness, and it is important to express it and let it go in order to reach the joy that lies underneath. It is precisely the suppression of these feelings of defeat and futility that lead to numbness. Becoming numb may reduce our awareness of pain but it also diminishes our passion for life. When we suppress our feelings, it is usually because they are too painful to face. We then deny that it matters to us that we got hurt or did not get what we wanted.

This suppression of feelings is often the underlying cause of depression. When any one feeling is suppressed, many other feelings are inevitably suppressed at the same time. If you are chronically or occasionally depressed, you may be suppressing something that matters to you, the importance of which you have denied on the surface. What feeling have you pushed down? What hurt or betrayal have you tried to ignore or cancel out as unimportant when, in fact, it matters deeply to you? No matter how trivial or unjustified your feelings might seem to be, allow yourself to explore them. If you are angry, this is usually a key to an underlying hurt. Explore the anger by expressing it out loud to yourself or writing in a journal until you can get to your true feelings beneath it.

Suppressed feelings can relate back to early childhood, or can be as recent as yesterday's meeting. Usually, if we are denying feelings that originate in our past, these same feelings can be triggered by individuals or situations in the present. They may relate to a parent's neglect, unfulfilled dreams, or broken promises. Take a look at all the things you feel you have missed out on in the past. Let yourself feel the sadness of not having found happiness or fulfillment. Magnify the feelings and go out of your way to identify all the aspects of yourself that fell short of your potential. What were your dreams? What did you long for in relationships? What had you hoped to achieve in your career?

Only by fully expressing suppressed grief can you break through the layers of numbness to find the rest of you—and probably the best of you.

When emotions are withheld, we also suffer physically. The natural flow of energy throughout the body becomes restricted, resulting in feelings of lassitude and fatigue, which perpetuate the cycle. Stemming the flow within us also stems the flow of energy in our external lives, interrupting the natural cycle of giving and receiving. We often instinctively limit or reduce our physical activity precisely so that the emotions inside do not get stirred up. In doing so, we are also inhibiting our breathing. Shallow breaths limit our emotional and physical experience, preventing us from fully accessing and cleansing our body and heart.

If it is difficult to overcome your numbness and access deeply buried emotions, move your body aerobically so that the feelings are forced to the surface. This will require conscious effort and determination, as the wounded emotional body will naturally resist being reawakened. Being your own best friend and having compassion for all that you have been through will help. The body, like the heart, must be loved back to life.

Being in the grey zone means that we have kept love in limbo, stopping the natural flow of abundance, in all its forms. Our passion peters out. We cease to believe or trust that we deserve happiness and love, and that the universe will provide either one. We therefore cease to trust and believe in ourselves and in others. By putting our love in limbo, we prevent ourselves and others from having it, and we effectively say "no" to receiving it. We make a decision that it is not available to us, and live our lives accordingly.

If it is difficult to overcome your numbness and access deeply buried emotions, move your body aerobically so that the feelings are forced to the surface.

Passion fruits

Whereas being in the grey zone is what happens when you allow life to just 'come at you', being passionate is what results when you actively make life happen. Passion is a pure, undiluted feeling with a powerful energetic charge behind it. It is usually the outcome of you embracing your personal power and expressing yourself—creatively, verbally or physically—in some heartfelt way, and it can be powerful enough to inspire or motivate others to act or change as well. It can also be the result of a realization, a discovery or an emotion that ignites a spark of feeling or conviction in you and prompts you to do something spontaneous or creative.

Passion is an expression of your unique essence—the deepest parts of yourself that make your personality unique—and it is your unique translation of life into joy.

But how do you create or access passion in your life? You cannot buy it and you cannot fake it. However, you can cultivate it and encourage it to come out. Being passionate means having an open heart and expressing your authentic self with creativity, spontaneity and love. It usually also implies breaking certain rules and allowing yourself to do something new or daring.

What you are passionate about in life usually distinguishes you from others. It lifts you out of the collective 'system' and transports you to a world where extra-ordinary things become possible, thanks to the powerful energetic force that your passion creates.

Pathways to passion:

- *dance or vigorous aerobic exercise that stimulates your body and stirs up emotions*
- *music that touches your heart or gets your body moving*
- *meditation in an environment that helps you get back in touch with yourself*
- *reconnecting with nature by walking in the woods, near water or up a mountain*
- *mixing with people, reading books or visiting museums or art galleries that relate to your area of passion to stimulate your creative juices and inspire new ideas.*

The grey zone then becomes an area of self-fulfilling prophecy—a realm of certainties preordained by our negative expectations. We get exactly what we are afraid of getting, and then we get even more of it to confirm what we always believed to be true.

Leaving the grey zone requires making a conscious decision to embrace life, and to allow yourself to fully express who you are and what you were meant to be.

Failing to do so not only drapes a huge grey cloud over your life, but over the lives of others also. And, likewise, choosing to come out from under that cloud not only makes you shine but also brings radiance to those around you.

To help lift that cloud, try experimenting with your spontaneity. Notice whenever you get a thought or idea about doing something, and catch yourself before your mind argues it out of existence. For example, if you like the idea of going for a walk on the beach, but your mind says it might rain, or you don't have time, just grab your coat and leave. Don't wait for the arguments to take root and immobilize you. Simply do it. At first, it may be a mindless exercise, devoid of feeling, but the more you allow yourself to act upon your impulses, the more feeling and pleasure will be generated.

Other creative spontaneous acts might include buying a card for someone who helped you, or sending flowers to someone who is ill. Or you might give some money to a homeless person on the street. These acts are an acknowledgement of life and your value in it. The important thing to remember is not to suppress any impulses or urges to do something. The feeling behind the impulse will be very fleeting at first because your mind has probably become very skilled at jumping in and squashing any attempts at spontaneous self-expression and passion. You must therefore take action as soon as you have the impulse. With practice, the impulses will become stronger, and the rewards of acting upon them will be greater.

When feelings are expressed and the body is reactivated physically and energetically, our creativity comes to life. Ideas come, wanting to be born. Dreams re-surface, wanting fulfillment. But remember: no one can pull you out of the grey zone. Only *you* have the power to say "yes" to life by loving yourself out of limbo.

Passion is your unique translation of life into joy.

Avoiding potential pitfalls

- ***Don't let yourself stay stuck in numbness.*** *Move. Breathe. Find ways to stir up your emotions and then express and resolve them so that they no longer weigh you down or keep you stuck.*
- ***Don't let all your decisions be purely logical, based on what is sensible, practical or financially wise.*** *Allow your heart to have its say and allow yourself to explore your dreams, regardless of what logic might dictate.*
- ***Remember that you are not alone.*** *There is a powerful universal force ready to co-create with you when you choose to move forward. Ask for help, take a risk, dare to shine and get yourself noticed, and the universe will support you.*

Chapter 6

The neediness cycle

If we love to be needed, we are nowhere near love at all.

Often we go into relationships without prior agreements and without deciding in advance what we want to get out of them. Instead, we have hopes and expectations, based on our needs, dreams and ideals. If these expectations are not met, we may become resentful and make our love conditional.

Expectations arise out of our missing pieces, creating emotional needs. This leaves little room for acceptance or for the freedom to be yourself. These kinds of needs, which usually date back to childhood, can never be met by your partner. Unless they are taken care of by you, they will push away potential partners. Any relationship that is not working is almost certainly founded on need, rather than on love.

It is sometimes difficult to distinguish need from love because they are so closely intertwined in childhood. When fundamental emotional needs are not met by our parents, having them met later in life is bound to feel good. This can mean that individuals feel temporarily fulfilled by meeting the needs of others and, in the process, seeming to be needed by them. The need to be needed, based on the belief that love must be earned, can become the dominant dynamic in a co-dependent relationship. In a sense, the need is being taken care of in this way, but the deeper underlying desire for balanced, wholesome love remains unfulfilled.

There are several things that can happen when we go into relationships with unmet needs. Firstly, the need or missing piece leads to a particular expectation of our partner, which creates pressure for him or her. If our partner fails to meet this need, we tend to retreat. This usually leads to resentment on our part, causing us to project onto our partner some justification as to why our need should be met, or the reason for it not being met. This, in turn, results in a power struggle, in which neither party gets what he or she wants, and no one is happy. The emotional need (missing piece) remains unfulfilled, intensifying and growing each time this happens (see illustration opposite).

Secondly, our need distorts our perception and makes us willing to settle for less than what we truly want. As a result, we often overlook basic—and sometimes glaring—incompatibilities. Declaring what we want, at the outset of a relationship, could (in our minds) jeopardize our chances of getting what we so badly need, and so we often say nothing and just hope for the best. It is an emotional trade-off that is guaranteed to backfire unless the cycle is broken.

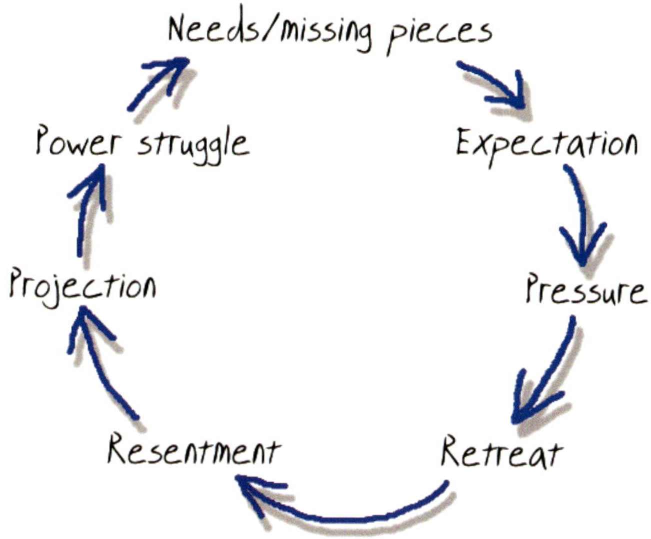

Thirdly, if we manage to take care of certain needs but not others, we run the risk of falling into the same trap all over again.

Françoise is a perfect example of this. Her husband of 12 years never gave her the affection and support she needed. To compensate, she poured her love into their children, making their needs more important than hers. She convinced herself that running the entire household single-handedly was not so bad because she was a good organizer and liked making order out of chaos. Finally, affection came to her in the form of a close male friend, and she realized what she had been missing and just how much it mattered. She left her husband for the other man. But, three years later, when her divorce was about to go through, she was suddenly wracked with doubts and started having panic attacks. Maybe she should go back to her husband. She missed the companionship she had felt with him. She mourned the fact that her marriage had not worked and that maybe she had not done enough to fix it. These thoughts haunted her and made her doubt her decision. Although her new partner brought her the affection and support she had been missing before, he still did not represent the ideal partner; other pieces were missing. As a result, she found herself trying to choose between two imperfect options, unable to conceive of a third—the ideal partner, with all the qualities that she wanted. Other missing pieces (such as self-respect and self-worth) prevented her from seeing that she deserved to have it all.

There is no avoiding the truth of our mastery: we are the ones who, through fear, need or desire, create the scenarios that we call life.

Needing leading nowhere

Ivan (32) was an engineer with a great deal of untapped potential. Every time he got into a relationship, however, he surrendered his own needs to take care of his partner. Not surprisingly, he attracted women who wanted a man to take care of them. Lisa was the latest in a long string of these. When Ivan met her, he fell in love with her vulnerability and immediately wanted to protect and care for her. His focus shifted from himself to her. Lisa loved all the attention and claimed she could do nothing without Ivan's help or input.

It was a perfect symbiosis, except that neither one of them was moving forward with their life or growing as individuals. Ivan's work suffered and he failed to follow through on several projects that he had been developing for months. Lisa relaxed into a life of easy comfort, doing nothing to explore her own potential or support Ivan in pursuing his dreams.

Both partners were avoiding taking responsibility for themselves by focusing on the other. It didn't take very long for a cycle of resentment and disillusionment to develop. Ivan eventually ended the relationship, exhausted from trying to meet Lisa's growing list of needs, at the expense of his own fulfillment.

Your 'missing pieces' are what you seek in your partner

By filling in your 'missing pieces', you can break cycles of co-dependence or neediness. When you remember that your partner usually has the same missing pieces as you, then you understand that he or she cannot give you something that neither of you ever had. You also realize that he or she is the most perfect mirror for showing you exactly what is missing within yourself.

Positive cycles

Once you start to give yourself what you have been trying to get from your partner, several things will happen. Firstly, your need will be diminished and you will be more able to unconditionally love and accept your partner. This means that there will be no pressure or expectation from you and, consequently, no reason for your partner to retreat and become resentful. It gives him or her the space to love you, and the freedom to choose that. By not projecting your need to be loved, you are transmitting a very different message about your 'lovability'. You are acting like a person who is already full of love, and therefore leave yourself open to being freely loved by others, without any pressure from you. Secondly, you will be teaching yourself something you were never taught while, at the same time, teaching it to your partner. By consciously providing what is missing, you create a cycle of positive growth so that your relationship with yourself and with your partner becomes more complete.

The need to be right

In power struggles, we often get side-tracked by another strong need—the need to be right. If we have had a highly disciplined upbringing, much of our parents' expression of love may have come in the form of rules and high standards. This kind of rigidity is often an expression of our parents' own love-deprived upbringing. It creates in them the need for control and in us a need for validation. Only by seeming to be right can we redeem our battered self-esteem. In our need to be right, we are trying to be acceptable as much to ourselves as to others. But in striving to be right, our arguments are often based on what we have been taught about ourselves, and they can be a way of rationalizing the way we behave.

Needing to be right therefore perpetuates the cycle. If you find yourself needing to be right in an argument, remember that that need is, in turn, based on a need for acceptance or love. Being right usually feels good because it validates us, but *needing* to be right can hinder our happiness because we then make others wrong. Understanding and letting go of the need to be right gives us the freedom to focus instead on validating ourselves, rather than trying to make ourselves complete through validation from others. Becoming complete through self-awareness and self-responsibility is an important pathway to happiness. And when we achieve this level of contentment, it not only feels much better than being right, but being right no longer matters.

self-responsibility

This is the key to breaking the neediness cycle and to creating a life of conscious choice and emotional freedom. Being responsible for ourselves is our most fundamental duty as individuals. The umbilical cord is cut when we are born and, after 18–20 years of training in basic life skills by our parents, we are set free to be all that we can be. Each of us is a distinct and separate individual—a single unit of self-sufficiency designed to breathe, talk, walk, live, love and choose on our own.

Taking responsibility for ourselves means:

- *not blaming others for the way life goes;*
- *making choices based on what we want or believe, rather than on others' expectations or standards;*
- *being committed to resolving our issues so that they do not result in projections, unhealthy needs or dysfunctional cycles in our relationships with others; and*
- *using our gifts and fulfilling our unique potential as powerful, creative beings.*

Needing to be right is based on the need for acceptance.

Needful love—a delicate balancing act

Ironically, the very person we depend on to meet our needs is usually the very person we refuse to allow into our hearts. While we may desperately want their love and affection, our fear of having it can prevent us from allowing it in. For if we had it, it would be so unfamiliar to us and so alien to our programming about ourselves that we would probably not know what to do with it. What we most want—love—is what we most fear if we do not believe we deserve it.

Many individuals who claim to want greater commitment in their relationship (yet repeatedly choose partners who are far from ready to commit to them) would run a mile if that partner were to suddenly turn around and ask them to get married. The dynamic is perfect: we can safely claim to want something (and endlessly bemoan the fact that we do not get it) when we attract a partner who is completely incapable of giving it to us. Attracting such a partner usually means that we ourselves are missing that very same ingredient.

An abrupt reversal of the neediness cycle can create emotional havoc, providing an opportunity to heal our love-deprived hearts by forcing us to deal with the emotional conflict that would result if we were suddenly showered with love. This would topple the delicate balance we had so carefully constructed: *you take care of me and I'll take care of you; let's not dig too deep and risk upsetting this comfortable arrangement.* But, of course, it is not at all comfortable, and it is only a matter of time before one partner tires of the game and the balancing act no longer works.

At the deepest level, however, both partners actually do need each other, as they are a perfect 'match'; for it is only through their needy relationship that they have the opportunity to discover what is missing within themselves and what they must do in order to break free of the neediness cycle.

When the chips are down...

Joan, aged 41, had a deep-seated need for love and affection, which she never got from her mother. This need resulted in her eating three large bags of potato chips every day. Feeling unfulfilled inside, she tried to fill the gnawing emptiness with comfort foods.

But each time Joan got into a relationship, she played out the same scenario with her partner. Just as one bag of chips was never enough for her to feel sated, she needed an excessive amount of her partner's time and energy. Her overwhelming neediness always pushed her partner away, reinforcing in her the deep-seated belief in her own 'unlovability' and thus intensifying her unmet need.

Joan had to learn to understand the source of her insatiable hunger. By acknowledging that the projection of her need onto her partner was perpetuating her cycle, she began to see that only she could meet her emotional need. Each time she reached for the bag of chips, she reminded herself that it was in reaction to her trigger of 'unlovability' (unworthiness/unacceptability), and that she was actually making herself less 'lovable' by smothering her partner and gaining weight. By demanding so much love and attention from him, she was giving him the message that she did not deserve his love.

Joan had to work at filling in her missing pieces of acceptance, respect and love, on a daily basis.

Many of us go to great lengths to avoid taking responsibility for our own lives and making a success of them. We are masterful at creating very 'legitimate' circumstances to justify our inaction: we need to help a friend who depends on us, we have had bad luck in business, or we don't have enough money or opportunities to do what we want. All of these and many more have been used to explain away a life put on hold. Yet there is no avoiding the truth of our mastery: we are the ones who, through fear, need or desire, create the scenarios that we call life.

Avoiding potential pitfalls

- ***Don't blame others for what is missing in your life.*** *Remember where the true power lies—inside you—and use it (in healthy, responsible ways) to get what you want. Your challenges represent the flip side of your power.*
- ***Don't fall into the trap of focusing on your partner's shortcomings.*** *This will distract you from your own and from the fact that his or her apparent shortcomings almost certainly reflect what is missing in you.*
- ***Don't get caught up in arguments based on your need to be right.*** *Recognize when and how your argument is based on the need for acceptance or validation. Practise filling in those missing pieces for yourself whenever a discussion or argument occurs.*

Chapter 7

Feeding the need

For as long as recreational drugs, comfort foods or sex make you feel better than you alone can make yourself feel, you will never be the best that you can be.

Comfort foods can seem like an attractive—and sometimes the only—option when your hunger for love has not been addressed or when emotional or physical pain becomes too much to handle.

Foods provide a pleasurable, if momentary, distraction from stress or distress, yet their effects can linger long after they have been ingested. Eating our favourite foods to blot out pain does a number of things. It gives a feeling of fullness, which may temporarily mask an emotional emptiness. It may bring some moments of happiness, from the sheer pleasure of eating something that tastes good. It may suppress emotions that we are not ready or willing to examine. And it may be part of a cycle of self-hatred, whereby depression over an overweight body can lead to further indulgence. Whatever the case, this kind of eating takes us deeper into our problems and prevents us from exploring solutions.

To break this cycle, a two-phased approach may be used. Begin by modifying the nature of what you eat. If, for example, you crave pastries when you are feeling down, try replacing them with something slightly more wholesome—such as a wholegrain equivalent, a cereal bar, or some other snack that will still give you the sweetness and carbohydrates you crave, but none of the fat or refined starches. In other words, maintain your habit, but try to progressively re-train your taste buds by switching from rich, sweet things to slightly less sweet, lower-calorie foods (see 'Ten tips for conscious eating', page 68). Although very unappealing at the beginning, this switch in taste and texture will eventually pay off and you will find yourself enjoying the healthier alternatives.

This is an important process (as much on the emotional level as on the physical) because you are very consciously re-programming your body. You are consciously deciding what to feed yourself and no longer mindlessly stuffing yourself with the very foods that will make you look and feel heavy and unhealthy. In doing so, you are creating a positive shift in your sense of self-worth, which will have a positive impact in other areas of your life. If you persevere, you will also begin to look and feel better. You are then ready to start the second phase.

Make a deal with yourself. Tell yourself you can still have your 'fix', but only after you have taken time to explore some of the issues that you have been trying to avoid. You may even buy or prepare your favourite food and have it sitting in front of you on the table as you do this. But do not touch it until you have taken a full 15 minutes to examine your issues.

Focus on your abdomen and try to determine what you are feeling there. Ask yourself what that feeling is related to. Is it to do with your appearance, your job, your relationship (or lack of one), your children, your family or your financial situation? Is it deeply buried grief, the loss or rejection of a loved one, or some other wound that has not been healed? Whatever the cause, try to identify it and trace it back as far as you can. When you have done this, try to sum it up in one or two sentences. What is the issue? What 'missing piece' might be driving this need? When you have identified some of the factors involved, find some way of moving energetically—running up and down stairs, jumping or jogging on the spot, or simply vigorously shaking your body while standing. Do this for two or three minutes and then close your eyes and feel the effect. Breathe deeply and think about your issue again. What could you possibly do to resolve it? How could you start to fill in your missing piece? What one positive single step could you take today towards a solution? Identify one thing and commit to doing it. If some emotions come up as a result of this, do not shove them back down so that you can indulge. Respect them, give them air time and, if possible, express them, either by crying, shouting or using that energy to determine a plan of action for yourself.

Now you can have your reward. But notice how you feel as you eat it. If you have done the exercise faithfully, you will probably feel that your need to eat has been slightly diminished, and that you can eat less. Or you may feel that you do not want to eat at all—or can put off eating until later. If possible, take that positive step before you indulge in another comfort food, and repeat the process the next time you need that food 'fix'. As you continue with this exercise, you will be diminishing your need while also taking positive action to remedy your situation. Eliminating the 'fix' without taking care of the deeper emotional need would not be a long-term solution.

Acknowledging and understanding your need for comfort foods enables you to see the need for what it really is: the body's way of telling you that love is missing somewhere in your life.

Ten tips for conscious eating

Eating without a conscious awareness of what, or how much, you are eating can be prompted by many things (stress, fear, suppressed emotions, despair, pain, sadness or poor nutrition) and can quickly become the habit of a lifetime. It can often be a symptom—and a source—of unhappiness in your life, masking some deeper issues that are getting in the way of your fulfillment.

If you suspect that the way you eat is not healthy (or that you are living to eat, rather than eating to live), then the following guidelines may help you break free of your dysfunctional relationship with food, find out what lies beneath it, and create a healthier body and mind.

1. ***Eat slowly.*** *Even if you are gorging yourself on your favourite junk food, try to chew each mouthful slowly, savouring every bite. Try to identify what you feel when you resist the urge to eat faster. If you can sit with that feeling without immediately smothering it with food, you may get some insights into your need to over-indulge.*
2. ***Include some form of protein with each meal*** *(eggs, fish, chicken, lean red meat—preferably organic, for maximum flavour). Steam, grill or bake rather than frying in oil or batter. If you are a vegetarian, try some protein powder—in the form of a smoothie, with some natural yogurt, nuts and fresh berries. This will help to reduce your appetite and cravings for carbohydrates or sweets.*
3. ***Replace pastries or high-sugar snacks*** *with some exotic fruit, such as papaya or pineapple (high in digestive enzymes). Add some roasted almonds or seeds for crunchiness and taste. If you cannot live without chocolate, try switching to the dark, 70% cocoa variety and eat it with some roasted almonds, which will reduce your overall sugar consumption and help stabilize your energy levels. You may be surprised to discover that healthier foods can also be delicious.*
4. ***Don't let chronic cravings run your life.*** *If you crave sweet things and feel fatigued or depressed without them, you may have an overgrowth of intestinal candida (a fungus that thrives on sugar and carbohydrates). Consult a health professional for advice on an appropriate anti-candida programme.*
5. ***Avoid eating when you are preoccupied with other things****—such as when you are working or on the move. Put everything else aside and focus on what you are eating. If you are stressed, tired, rushed or otherwise distracted, your body cannot do a good job of processing what you eat and your food is likely to end up causing indigestion or being stored as fat.*
6. ***Start your day with a glass of unchilled mineral water*** *and try to drink at least six more glasses during the day. This will help your body to flush out toxins and to reduce your cravings for processed foods.*
7. ***Eat light at night.*** *The evening is often the time when we most feel like indulging (out of boredom, loneliness or a need for comfort). It is also the time when we can do the most damage, since our digestive system slows down when we sleep and therefore cannot adequately process our food. As a result, we may feel sluggish and 'hung over' the morning after a late-night binge, craving a quick pick-me-up in the form of carbohydrates (bread, croissants, sugared cereal), which only perpetuates the 'fast food'* cycle.*
8. ***Listen to your body.*** *It is your best friend, despite the neglect or abuse that you may have inflicted upon it over the years. It holds the key to balance in your life and it will always tell you when you are going against what is best for you. It knows when you have eaten enough or if you have eaten the wrong things, and it*

will tell you by making you feel uncomfortable, listless or fatigued. If you are eating unconsciously, it is likely that some emotions are being suppressed and that more than purely physical nourishment is required. If, for example, affection and support are missing in your life, you may subconsciously be trying to compensate with food, rather than addressing the deeper issues. Try to feel your emotions when you find yourself reaching for comfort foods and explore the possible reasons for these feelings. Respect and befriend your body and it will become your partner in creating what you want.

9. ***Give your body a break.*** *You may be frustrated with your world, your circumstances or your body, but your body is not to blame. It has done its utmost to sustain you, despite your neglect or over-indulgence, and it deserves your full and loving attention. It may require some tender loving care in order to regain a healthy balance. If you can muster the discipline and the willingness to make even some minor healthy adjustments, you will see a difference in your life. You may not initially be motivated to make these changes but, if you do, you will not regret it. Being good to your body not only helps you to feel better about yourself but also usually attracts the very things that you lack and are trying to compensate for with food.*

10. ***Relax.*** *If you need to eat but are stressed, emotionally upset or short of time, try not to abuse your body further by forcing it to process food on top of everything else. If you do not have enough time to exercise and work off some of the stress or emotional buildup, take some deep breaths and do some simple exercises (such as bending forward to touch your toes then leaning backwards, hands in the air, or jogging on the spot). This will aerate your body and help to release any pent-up energy. You will then be more able to consciously choose what to eat, or to postpone eating until you are more relaxed.*

Foods that nourish and sustain the body

- *Whole grains, such as brown rice, buckwheat and rye*
- *Good-quality protein (e.g., free-range eggs, fish)*
- *Organic vegetables, steamed or baked*
- *Nuts and seeds, fresh and lightly roasted*
- *Hempseed powder (rich in essential fatty acids)*
- *Natural yogurt (which is good for the intestines)*
- *Fresh fruit (particularly blueberries, cherries, pineapple, papaya and red grapes)*
- *Natural mineral water and sea salt (for trace minerals)*
- *Vinaigrette made with apple cider vinegar and olive oil*
- *Wholesome snacks, such as nut/seed bars*
- *Red wine, in moderation*
- *Organic dark chocolate, in moderation*

Foods that deplete or damage the body

- *Processed foods (e.g., packaged cereals and soups)*
- *Refined starches and sugars, such as cakes, pastries, white bread, white pasta, white sugar and sweets*
- *Fried or deep-fried foods and hydrogenated oils*
- *Artificial sweeteners, such as aspartame*
- *Dairy products, when eaten in excess (particularly cream, high-fat cheeses and yogurts high in sugar)*
- *Animal fat, such as lard and fatty meat*
- *Carbonated drinks that are high in sugar*
- *Alcohol, when consumed in excess*

* *Whereas wholesome food (i.e., food in its natural, unprocessed form) is digested slowly and yields vital nutrients for sustained energy and health, most processed foods are high in simple carbohydrates or sugars that are quickly processed and used up by the body. 'Fast foods' can therefore cause a rapid rise in blood sugar levels, followed by a sudden drop; this can leave us feeling depleted and in need of more fast-energy foods, creating a cycle of dependence.*

This information serves as a general guide and is not intended as a substitute for medical treatment, where required. Consult a health professional for specific advice on your individual needs.

Chapter 8

The compensation factor—our emotional 'first-aid kit'

Human beings, by changing the inner attitudes of their minds, can change the outer aspects of their lives.
—William James

Nature abhors a vacuum, and the void created by every essential formative quality that we did not receive as children (such as love, support and affection), must be filled with something else.

We naturally compensate for any essential aspects of love that we do not receive as children. If, for example, we did not get support, we might become fiercely independent—often to the point where we rarely allow others to help us. This is our instinctive reaction to an initial hurtful experience of rejection. It becomes our survival technique or coping mechanism for ensuring that we do not get hurt again.

Although such coping mechanisms may serve us well in dealing with emotional shortfalls, they can also become a means of distancing and disconnecting ourselves from others. Because these mechanisms develop in reaction to an unmet need, every time that same need surfaces in life we tend to revert to that same form of compensation. For example, those who compensated for a lack of love by becoming fiercely independent, bring in this same quality whenever love threatens to overwhelm them with its power to open the heart. Opening to love would mean being vulnerable, and their subconscious remembers all too well what that led to in the past. It learned that the only way to survive was to be strong and to avoid any dependence on others. However, holding on to this mechanism means that their painful past is projected into an unknown, scary future, and the cycle continues.

Compensation strategies can sometimes be highly beneficial in one's career. They can result in the development of finely honed skills that influence an individual's career choices and degree of success. An extremely independent young girl could, for example, develop into a tough, highly successful businesswoman. However, it is when the independence overflows into one's personal life, acting as a protective barrier rather than an asset, that the compensation strategy becomes an obstacle to personal fulfillment.

Being able to distinguish when it is or is not appropriate and constructive to apply one's strategies is the key to ensuring that they remain a positive asset.

The three stages of compensation

Several levels of compensation develop throughout our formative years. By looking at our essential needs as we develop and grow, it is possible to determine our individual compensation strategies.

1. Childhood

In childhood, our greatest need is usually the security and comfort of parental love and affection. When this is missing, we need to find some way to make ourselves feel secure, safe and somehow comforted. Becoming withdrawn, a pleaser or fiercely independent are some of the most common forms of compensation at this age. Some develop dissociative tendencies whereby they create other 'selves' in their minds for comfort. In extreme cases, this can lead to Multiple Personality Disorder.

It is in these early childhood years (from birth to about seven years of age), that the seeds of one's reactive 'life cycles' are sown. Few psychologists or medical doctors today would dispute the concept that love is life-giving nourishment, as essential for the physical body as the food we need in order to grow. The strongest expression of love is in the form of touch, a sensitivity for which our skin is uniquely designed. Touch acts as the connector between mind and body, and it has a deep and powerful effect on our psyche. Emotional (sensory) malnourishment therefore leads to physical, as well as emotional, imbalances. Often what appear to be genetically inherited conditions or diseases are, in fact, the same 'missing pieces' that have been handed down from generation to generation. Parents can only teach what they have learned, and their own unresolved 'missing pieces' inevitably get passed on to their offspring.

Although the compensatory traits may be easy to spot in one's behaviour (once you go looking for them), they often have a deeper emotional impact that may not become apparent for decades.

It is in childhood that the seeds of one's reactive 'life cycles' are sown.

Peer pressure is intense for adolescents and many individuals distort themselves in order to be 'okay'. If they do not fit in with their peers, they must come up with a strategy for coping with this rejection.

Other possible compensation strategies of this first phase include tenacity, pragmatism, habitual emotional detachment, and heightened sensitivity or observation skills.

2. Adolescence

The second significant phase of our development occurs in our teens, when one of the biggest issues is usually acceptance—fitting in, being accepted as part of a group. Peer pressure is intense at this time, and many individuals distort themselves in order to be 'okay'. If they do not fit in with their peers, at school or socially, they may feel the need to come up with a strategy for coping with this rejection. Being unacceptable to one's peers can often result in teenagers focusing their energies inwards in an attempt to see what is 'wrong' with them. This introspection can, in turn, result in the individual becoming highly perceptive and aware, if somewhat withdrawn from society. Those who react this way often become perfectionists and analytical in outlook. They may also become highly intellectual, having used their minds to devise complex defence mechanisms and survival skills.

If individuals are considered to be physically unacceptable by their peers, they may compensate by becoming either neutral or flamboyant in their dress and personal presentation. If, for example, a young teenage girl perceives that her expression as a woman is unacceptable, she may react by dressing down or neutrally so that she becomes sexless and less visible as a woman. If she feels she is being rejected because she feels ugly, she may react by becoming outlandish in the way she dresses, developing her own unique style to detract attention from her physical self, and to make it impossible for her to be compared with her peers.

Other possible compensation strategies in this second phase include the tendency to be rebellious, individualistic, critical/judgemental or ingratiating (a pleaser).

3. Adulthood

As teenagers enter adulthood, their greatest needs often include validation and encouragement, which they require in order to confidently express themselves and carve out their niche in the world. If they do not receive this validation from those who matter in their lives, they may react by becoming subservient, overly diligent, workaholics or reckless—depending on how they compensated in the previous two stages. They may even become saboteurs, unable or unwilling to hold down a job because they hold a grudge against the world for not acknowledging their achievements.

The package that results from this compensation process is like a personal 'first-aid kit'. It is used to protect, defend and guard against the kind of hurtful experiences that led to the development of these strategies in the first place. It also serves as a comfort and refuge—a place where you retreat to console yourself and justify your behaviour as being the only rational option in the circumstances. But by guarding the self and justifying the strategy, individuals ensure that they never get what they want. Their compensation strategy gets in the way of their ability to be spontaneous, natural, open—and honest with themselves. They therefore set themselves up for an illusory and convoluted world. They may still have a deep-seated need for the essential components that they did not receive earlier in life, but they will probably also have a fear of obtaining them, based on their low self-worth. The fear is always accompanied by a need for the very thing that the strategy is designed to protect against.

The inevitable outcome is that individuals attract the circumstances and relationships that trigger these same fears and needs, leading them to justify the continued need for their 'first-aid kit'. The cycle becomes so convoluted and complex that individuals rarely see it for what it is—an elaborate cover-up scheme that keeps a part of them hidden and inaccessible.

The cycle becomes so convoluted and complex that individuals rarely see it for what it is—an elaborate cover-up scheme that keeps a part of them hidden and inaccessible.

The following exercise enables you to identify your compensation strategies so that you can avoid using them inappropriately.

Exercise 5

What I didn't get during...	***What I compensated with:***
1. Childhood	
e.g.: Affection, hugs	*e.g: Independence, aloofness*
2. Adolescence	
e.g.: Acceptance by the 'in' crowd at school	*e.g: Perfectionist tendencies, top grades*
3. Adulthood	
e.g.: Encouragement/validation at work	*e.g.: Conscientiousness at work to earn praise*

4. When do you come up against these same needs in your relationships, work or family?

It is at these times that you automatically slip into your compensatory behaviour for fear of suffering the same painful experience as before. Because your missing pieces attract situations and relationships that trigger these same sensitive issues, you will tend to use your 'first-aid kit' often and subconsciously. Look at its three main components and try to determine how you use them in your relationships.

Whenever you use your 'first-aid kit', remember what caused you to develop it. Your 'first-aid kit' may be saving you in apparent 'emergencies', but it may also be stopping you from getting what you have been missing all your life.

To ensure that these strategies are only used constructively in your life, first determine which three are dominant in your personal 'first-aid kit'. Once you have identified these, you can begin to examine the ways in which you apply them in your personal life. For example, if your kit consists of fierce independence, perfectionist/critical tendencies, and emotional detachment, look at your relationships—either past or present—to see how and when these strategies surface.

If you find yourself switching off emotionally whenever intimacy is a possibility, for example, you can be sure that your strategy is surfacing to 'protect' you from the 'threat' of closeness. There may be several ways of creating that emotional detachment—for example, finding fault with your partner so that an argument ensues, or becoming caught up in the detail of perfecting something so that you are distracted or end up too tired. Not feeling well may be another way of keeping your distance. Filling in your missing pieces helps to defuse such strategies, but understanding how and why they developed enables you to more readily 'catch yourself at your own game'.

Once you recognize just how much these strategies are preventing you from getting what you want out of life, you may become more willing to give up the need to be right. However, since the strategies were developed by the ego to keep you 'safe', they are not easily relinquished. Deciding that you want to be happy more than you want to be right is essential to breaking out of this cycle.

Avoiding potential pitfalls

- ***Don't let your professional strengths affect your personal relationships.*** *Catch yourself when you find that you are using your skills to manipulate or take control of a situation. If you are relating to your partner with cold detachment, this is a sure sign that you are using your 'first-aid kit'.*
- ***Don't retreat into the safety of your mind.*** *If you find yourself over-analysing things in your head, stop yourself and try to connect in some meaningful way. Try to adopt a beginner's mind, even if you think you know all the answers. Dare to leave your comfort zone and risk being vulnerable by asking for input or expressing your feelings.*
- ***Don't deflect compliments or other forms of praise that come your way.*** *This diminishes your self-worth and leaves no room for you to receive. Even though it may feel uncomfortable at first, simply say "thank you" until that becomes your natural, genuine response.*

Chapter 9

Looking for evidence

Growth is the only evidence of life.
—John Henry Newman

When the foundation of our personality is laid down in childhood, we see ourselves as having a particular place and value in the world. Depending on our missing pieces, we subconsciously take on various roles—the role of pleaser, leader, crusader, follower, doormat, etc. Because, as children, we see our limited family world as absolute, we assume that our particular role applies as much in the outside world as it does at home. What we are taught as children, we extrapolate into our adult lives.

What is familiar to us often feels safe, and our instinctive need for safety can mean that we have an investment in maintaining the status quo. Even if our assumed role in life is a negative one, involving low self-esteem or 'doormat' qualities, it forms the matrix of our early development and of our world. Our entire personality is usually built around this role, and we may subconsciously fear that we would crumble without it.

Because of this investment in maintaining our perceived role in life, whenever it is challenged we tend to look for evidence to prove that it is still valid.

Here's an example of how this can work:

Jane's partner, Chris, had a habit of forgetting to call when he got delayed at the office. This made Jane very angry because it made her feel insignificant in his life. It got to the point where, as soon as Jane got home each evening, she went straight to the answering machine to see if Chris had left a message—knowing in advance that he had not, and wanting to prove to herself that she was right. Respect and consideration were missing for Jane early in life and she subconsciously looked for evidence to prove that she did not deserve to have these qualities in her relationships. She wanted them, but at the same time she needed them not to be there so that her world remained familiar and made sense. By looking for evidence in this way, she perpetuated her cycle, reinforcing it with every scrap of evidence she found. The 'evidence' was plentiful because she had attracted a partner for whom respect and consideration had also been missing in his life. He was therefore the perfect mirror for Jane to see what was missing in her.

In observing how you look for evidence of your assumed status in life, remember that your partner can only behave the way he or she does if you continue to behave the way you do. Your expectation of, and need for, a certain outcome create the inevitable. When you find yourself looking for evidence, ask yourself the following questions: What is the belief that I'm subconsciously trying to prove is true? Do I need to be right about it? What do I stand to lose by giving it up? What do I stand to gain? How could I ask for what I need in a healthy, loving way?

There is always a cost and a payoff in perpetuating a dysfunctional cycle. Costs are high and usually include love, affection, intimacy, communication, honesty, good health and peace of mind. Payoffs or benefits include being right, being in control and a false sense of safety.

When the cost begins to outweigh the benefit, you are ready to let go of the need to be right. Old habits die hard, however, and you will need to catch yourself each time you start looking for evidence.

Remember, you are building a case against yourself—a case that you can continue winning, if you choose, because you are judge, jury and defendant. But winning this kind of case is a hollow—and usually solitary—victory. There are no awards for damages, and being right eventually becomes a poor substitute for being happy.

Avoiding potential pitfalls

- ***Don't fall into the trap of feeling vindicated if you find evidence to prove the validity of your suspicions.*** *You will simply have confirmed your amazing ability to attract circumstances that show you what you are missing inside.*
- ***Don't forget that looking for evidence keeps you stuck.*** *Put your energies into filling in your missing pieces rather than trying to blame the other person for not giving you what you want.*

To help you see how you go 'looking for evidence', identify any complaints or criticisms that you may have about your partner, following the example below.

Exercise 6

My complaints/criticisms:	*Missing piece:*
e.g.: I'm treated like a servant; my partner never does anything unless I ask him to.	*Support, respect*
______________________	______________________
______________________	______________________
______________________	______________________
______________________	______________________

Chapter 10

The limitations of labelling

What we think of others is relative to what we think of ourselves.

Another way of perpetuating our cycles is through labelling. We all readily and subconsciously attach labels to those in our life, judging them to be a certain way. But such labels can limit our chances of making a breakthrough in our relationship with them.

Consider the conclusions you have come to regarding some key individuals in your life. If your mother-in-law has a habit of trying to run your life, have you labelled her 'interfering', 'controlling' or worse? If your partner has let you down three times in a row, have you labelled him/her 'unreliable' or 'untrustworthy'?

Labelling is similar to looking for evidence, but its focus is reversed. Whereas gathering evidence involves subconsciously building a case against yourself, labelling involves building a case against someone else. It is an outward projection of what is missing inside. The mother-in-law's interference, for example, would be an outward projection and reflection of one's own sense of powerlessness or lack of assertiveness.

Whatever the label we affix to people, the result is always the same. It immediately reduces the possibility of our relationship with them ever improving. This is because we begin to act and think in accordance with the narrow parameters of the labels by which we have defined others.

Remember, it is usually only because we are critical of ourselves (believing ourselves to not be good enough, or to be wrong) that we attract others who reflect this back to us. In believing ourselves to not be good enough, for example, our performance often reflects our lack of self-confidence and can attract doubts or criticism as a result.

Every time we label someone, it is as if we 'write them off' in terms of their potential to be anything more than that. From our perspective, the label defines both how we perceive them relating to us, and our relationship to them. The label categorizes them as having a fixed way of being that leaves little room for a breakthrough. We set ourselves up for the kind of interaction that confirms our subconscious beliefs and expectations.

We may find ourselves saying, for example, "My mother will never agree to that because she is too old-fashioned",

Designer labels

Robert, a graphic designer, felt that his boss, George, was always finding fault with his work, and he had labelled him 'critical'. Whenever Robert contemplated a conversation with George, he automatically prepared for the criticism he expected to come his way. However, this made him defensive, which, in turn, often made him come across as if he had something to hide. The kind of conversation he had with George, then, was one in which George was critical and Robert was defensive, leaving little room for anything else. Ironically, although Robert was competent at his job, he often did less well than he could have, simply because the anticipated criticism made him feel that he could never be good enough. This affected his motivation and self-esteem and his performance inevitably suffered—generating more of the criticism he so feared.

In applying the critical label, Robert was also covering up for his own feelings of insecurity in his job. Despite his competence, he was not entirely self-confident. Labelling George 'critical' was his subconscious way of trying to convince himself and others that the reason for the criticism had nothing to do with him being inadequate; it was simply the result of a critical person—George—finding fault with him because it was in his boss's nature to be critical, and not because Robert actually deserved such criticism. The only way for Robert to break out of this cycle was to give George some positive new labels—such as 'supportive' and 'fair'—and to then respond to him as if his boss consistently exhibited those qualities.

or "My partner wouldn't trust me to go away on my own because he's very jealous". Who is deciding the outcome here, before the individual concerned even has a chance to have their say? In making such assumptions, we are also forgetting that the dynamics of our relationships are determined by how we relate to ourselves and, by extension, to all others.

To help break the cycle, identify what labels you have for those in your life. You may find yourself justifying your label for them, saying that they were like that before you ever met them, and that everyone else feels the same way about them. However, it is important to remember that you attracted these particular people into your life so that they could show you certain dynamics within yourself. Obtaining a consensus among your friends about the labels you attach to others is not proof of your appropriate

If we judge people according to who we are, and if who we are is determined by our missing pieces, then every time we label someone we reinforce our cycles.

What do your labels of others say about you?

labelling; it is merely testimony to your amazing ability to gather evidence (in the form of friends or circumstances) that support your own beliefs. Your labels are relative to who you believe yourself to be, and this image of yourself is supported and reflected back to you by those in your life. (See Exercise 7.) By changing the labels you attach to others, you enable them to relate differently to you. You, in turn, begin to relate differently to yourself.

Every time you interact with someone, mentally remove any negative or limiting labels you may have given them, replacing them with positive, compassionate labels, likely to foster acceptance, respect, trust and understanding, etc. Even attaching a new label to people and deciding to perceive them in a positive light is enough to start breaking your cycle. This not only generates and reinforces good relationships, but also creates break-throughs with those you may have 'written off' as being fixed in their ways or impossible to deal with. If someone is consistently late, for example, you may label them 'unreliable'. This may make you feel unimportant or disrespected, but it is important to remember that it is not just a matter of giving them a positive label and

Exercise 7

Labels I attach to others:	***What that says about me:***
e.g.: My mother is selfish	*I don't feel I deserve her attention (i.e., I'm unimportant)*
______________________	______________________
______________________	______________________
______________________	______________________
______________________	______________________
______________________	______________________
______________________	______________________
______________________	______________________

treating them accordingly. If the issue being triggered in you is one of respect, then you must practise respect for yourself and them by letting them know that it is not acceptable to always be late. If they continue to be late, nonetheless, then you might practise self-respect by not being there when they finally do turn up.

Use Exercise 8 to make a list of the positive labels you could attach to those same people featured on your list in Exercise 7. Identify how you intend to relate to them, in accordance with this positive label. Even though you may feel that they do not deserve to be treated nicely by you, remember that they are merely reflecting back to you what is missing within yourself. They are probably also missing this same quality in themselves, and are therefore unable to give it to you, no matter how much they might love or like you. You will therefore be doing yourself and them a favour by introducing this quality into your relationship. By rising above your need to have them be nice to you first, you are practising unconditional acceptance—a quality that will ultimately make you a happier, richer person.

Avoiding potential pitfalls

- ***Don't forget that making someone wrong does not make you right.*** *Labelling does not let you off the hook. It is merely a distorted projection of your own perceived limitations. Focus on having positive labels—for yourself and others—so that your communication with other people is equally positive.*
- ***Don't diminish or distort yourself to accommodate others' moods or aggressiveness.*** *This is an opportunity for you to strengthen those areas within yourself that are challenged by seemingly formidable individuals.*
- ***Resist the temptation to find other ways of categorizing people,*** *such as claiming to make charitable allowances for them because they are a certain way. You are still labelling them, and the effect will be the same—a missed opportunity for an unexpected outcome, and disempowerment on both sides.*

Exercise 8

Positive labels I can use:	***How my behaviour will change:***
e.g.: My mother is generous	*e.g.: I will treat her as if she has given me everything.*

Chapter 11

Focus and projection: reality perspectives

As a man is, so a man sees.
—William Blake

Most people live their lives reactively. They see themselves as being at the effect of others, obliged to react in certain ways. But these reactions are often based on survival strategies that enable them to remain within their comfort zone.

Our perspective is all-important in determining the extent and nature of our personal power. If we tend to focus on our external world and to see the events of our life as simply 'coming at us', beyond our control, we unwittingly relinquish our power to others. We set them up as the cause of what happens to us, and therefore can only react to what comes our way. This can make us feel vulnerable and defensive. It can also make us feel powerless to make a difference.

To maintain this perspective, a great deal of energy is required in order to assess and cope with what comes at us from the outside world. Constant monitoring and sensory perception are required to deal with the unexpected. For if we believe ourselves to be at the effect of an unpredictable world, there can never be a feeling of safety or inherent order. Insurance policies and alarm systems may seem to provide reassurance, but they are devices designed to deal with some outside force that we see as always potentially greater than we are. They can therefore never provide true inner security.

Our senses constitute our own personal radar, designed to keep us safe. However, we utilize them almost exclusively in our outward focus and projection. When we see something coming our way, whether it be in the form of an angry partner, an accident or some other threat, we usually react with our instinctive survival mechanisms. In this way, the outside world determines our behaviour and, therefore, our lives, and we are buffeted about by its seemingly random winds of change. We become reactive coping machines, adept in the art of survival, but poorly equipped to consistently and proactively thrive.

When this outward projection is reined in, and the senses and energy are instead focused inwards, the entire dynamic changes. Just as our outward focus on the world leads us to mould ourselves around it, an inward focus results in the outside world falling into place in accordance with our internal programming. This involves determining how we wish to feel at any given time, in any given situation. Rather than allowing outside circumstances to dictate our reaction, we can instead decide how we would ideally like to feel so that circumstances fall into place in accordance with our positive programming.

In essence, the world begins to respond to us, rather than us reacting to it. The dynamic is the same in either direction, and will work just as powerfully one way or the other, depending on our focus. It is simply a matter of deciding whether we wish to live a life of reaction or one of conscious proactivity. It is also, of course, a matter of acknowledging that we do, indeed, wield that much power.

The proof of such power comes quickly and easily, given the right focus. By simply deciding, in advance of a situation, how you wish to feel inside, you will begin to see your world respond to you differently. If, for example, you are anticipating a difficult conversation with someone, you might normally have focused on how you expected them to behave, visualizing their aggressiveness or anticipating their lack of cooperation. If, instead, you bring your focus inwards, and decide that you are going to feel harmonious, open, receptive, calm, relaxed, amenable, fulfilled, acknowledged and respected, then your conversation is likely to generate a much more positive outcome. Your demeanor, body language and energy field will broadcast these qualities, and your words and actions will come from within this positive context.

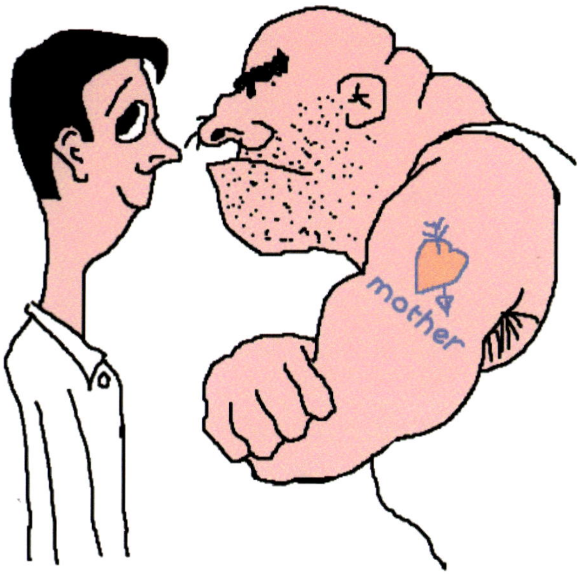

If you bring your focus inwards, your conversation is likely to generate a much more positive outcome.

Because our focus is a transmission of energy, focussing on the other person can seem to give them power over you; focussing on yourself not only brings that power and energy back to where it naturally belongs and resides—inside you—but also further defuses your triggers, reconnects you to yourself, and greatly enhances your ability to attract what you want.

Breaking the ice with Gloria

Joseph drove home from work at 5pm every day, passing by the old house on the corner where his neighbour Gloria lived. Known as the town grump, Gloria always sat on her doorstep in the late afternoon sunshine, glowering at passersby, and shouting at the kids playing on the street. She had no friends and never seemed to have a kind word for anyone. She was given a wide berth.

Having observed this for months, Joseph came to the conclusion that Gloria's life must have been filled with hardship and unhappiness. He decided to do something about it.

The following evening, as he passed by in his car, he rolled down his window and waved to Gloria, calling out her name and smiling broadly. Gloria's grumpy expression hardened and she glared at him with all the ferocity of her 65 years. For the next four days, Joseph repeated the routine, rolling down his window, calling out her name, and giving her his most captivating smile. No response. If anything, Gloria seemed to freeze when he approached, steeling herself against this invasion of her armour-plated defensiveness. Undeterred, Joseph repeated the process the following week, increasing his fervour, asking her how she was and wishing her a nice day.

On the Wednesday of the third week, it was a particularly hot day and Joseph drove home with the roof down. As he approached Gloria's place, he slowed almost to a stop, took both hands off the steering wheel, raised himself halfway out of his seat and waved exuberantly at her as he passed. "Hi, Gloria!" he yelled at the top of this lungs, beaming and flailing his arms. "Hope you had a great day, Gloria!"

A huge smile broke free from Gloria's frozen features, and a light came on in her eyes. Joseph was so overcome he almost crashed into the mailbox on the corner, and had to swerve to avoid it. This made Gloria double over with laughter, and it was as if the whole street had come to life. Intoxicated by her laughter, Joseph drove the rest of the way home in a daze, marvelling at what had happened. As a high-technology inventor, he had created many miraculous devices in his lifetime, but never had he felt such exhilaration. Making Gloria smile, after her decades of misery, was a breakthrough unlike any other. Only by persevering for almost three weeks had he managed to melt the ice around her heart.

Gloria was never the same again. She seemed to look forward to Joseph's return from work, leaning out over the steps, ready to wave and smile as he drove past. The kids on the street noticed the change too. They found her softer, and no longer felt the need to cross the street to avoid her. And she began to talk to them, her voice still gruff but her words not unkind.

A tiny community changed because one man believed in his ability to have a positive effect on those around him. He knew enough about love to understand how deeply it could be buried, and that excavating it took time and a strong conviction in one person's ability to have a powerful effect on another. Rather than being affected by Gloria's sadness, like everyone else on the street, Joseph instead chose to affect Gloria with his love and joy. She experienced the release that only persistent, unconditional love could bring. And Joseph knew the power and magic of believing in his ability to make a difference.

We need to constantly remind ourselves that we can and do have as much effect on our world as our world appears to have on us. However, in creating this shift of perspective, we must also be aware that there will appear to be resistance to the changes we try to implement. This is partly due to our own self-doubts, and is our subconscious way of testing ourselves. When we encounter such resistance, it is as if our subconscious mind is challenging us to stand our ground and demonstrate our conviction in what we are standing for. When we break the old rules and impose new ones, we are grappling simultaneously with the old self and the new, and we need to believe in ourselves firmly enough to break through the resistance and prove to ourselves that we are, indeed, who we are claiming to be.

The true story opposite illustrates the power of focus and projection, and the need to persist with our new way of being during that challenging period of resistance.

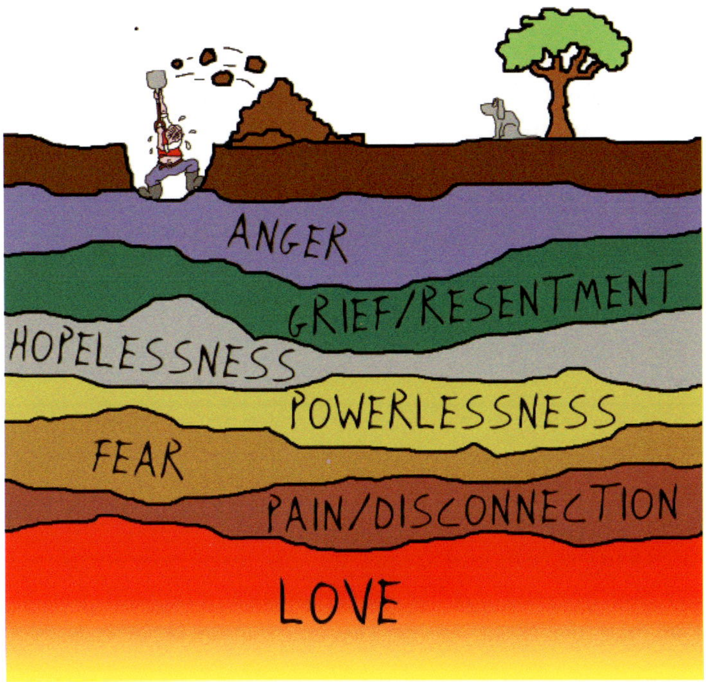

Avoiding potential pitfalls

- ***Don't be deceived by circumstances.*** *Remember that you created them. And only you have the power to change them, or adjust your life accordingly, if you do not like them.*
- ***Never underestimate your potential to make a difference.*** *You have skills, character traits, features, a voice and a personality that are unique to you. No one else has that particular combination; no one else can process or perceive the world the way you do. Trust the value of your uniqueness and use it at every opportunity.*
- ***Don't lose your focus.*** *Remember that the world responds to you when you focus on living your life proactively.*

How deeply do you dig to reach the love buried within yourself and within those around you? Do you care enough to keep digging?

Chapter 12

The power-struggle syndrome

Power is the effect we have on other people

We all have the potential to use our personal power to express our unique gifts and to change our world. Relationships are one of the most effective forums in which to do this, since our power is usually defined by how we relate to others. However, many of us fail to put this power to good use—often out of a fear of failure or an incomplete understanding of its nature and purpose.

Being empowered means being switched on and tuned in to who we really are. It means being connected on all levels so that our mental, emotional, physical and spiritual forces work together to create a positive outcome. If power is purely physical, it can be abusive and destructive. If it is merely emotional, it can be manipulative or based on need. If purely intellectual, it may be ego-driven, lacking in compassion or human kindness. And if purely spiritual, it may not be grounded in the real world or practically applicable in our lives.

Our fears often distort the expression of our personal power, causing us to limit the extent of our output or connections. But, whether we are aware of it or not, we are always wielding our power in some way and having an effect on others. Unless we are actively and consciously powerful, however, we cannot control the *kind* of effect we exert.

To be truly powerful, then, requires an understanding of the holistic nature of power and what we stand to gain—or lose—by fully exercising that power. It also requires taking responsibility for how we use our power.

Being consciously and deliberately powerful means affecting others through our manner of talking, behaving and directing our energy. This energy is transmitted in a variety of ways—through our eyes, body postures, actions, emotions and words.

We are all meant to be powerful. And if our power is not activated (manifesting itself as creativity, initiative, passion, inspiration or utilization of our unique gifts), then a vacuum is created. Life can start to implode, shrinking in size and scope. We may experience internal conflict because our life on the outside does not match the dynamic blueprint on the inside that is fighting to express itself.

Just as machines run less efficiently on half power, so too do human beings. When we diminish our personal power, we often end up suppressing our intuition and numbing ourselves to our intuitive guidance. Routine and predictability can then become the hallmarks of our existence.

This is the price we pay when our fears prevent us from fully embracing our power. We may prefer to sidestep the responsibility that goes with being truly powerful rather than facing the possibility of failing in our endeavours. By doing so, however, we miss out on the opportunity to experience one of the most exhilarating forces on earth—the force of the human heart. For that is where much of our power resides.

Our power cannot be taken against our will, for our will *is* our power. Focused willpower can create breakthroughs in our lives. When regularly directed towards a particular goal and combined with positive intent, inspiration and true desire, willpower can move mountains. It can bring about miraculous transformation. It can heal our bodies.

Empowerment is infectious. Others cannot fail to be touched by it. Conversely, the suppression of our own power may actually disempower others. By withholding from them the gift of our unique form of powerfulness, we diminish the quality and impact of our interactions, while retaining a certain control and avoiding the risk of failure. This is a distorted use of our power, but power nonetheless.

To avoid being truly powerful, we often convince ourselves that others have greater power over us. We may make decisions accordingly—saying, for example, that we will not take a certain course of action because a particular person would react negatively, or make us look foolish. We use their anticipated reactions or behaviour as a justification for not meeting our fears—and our

The price of disempowerment

June, aged 48, never did ask her boss for a raise because she was convinced he would say no and did not value her as an employee. She stayed where she was for another two years, disenchanted and unfulfilled, until her boss replaced her with someone more dynamic.

John, 34, would have loved to ask his girlfriend to marry him, but he was sure he would be rejected, and so he never popped the question. She left him for another man, claiming she wanted someone who was not afraid of commitment.

Marianne, 56, felt that all the passion had been leached out of her 26-year marriage. She desperately wanted to do some courses in personal development to find herself and to re-ignite all the passion inside her. But she was sure her husband, George, would object. George, profoundly depressed by his lacklustre marriage, and convinced that his wife no longer loved him, had an affair with his secretary and developed a serious drinking problem.

Playing safe did not pay off for any of these individuals. All three were far more likely to have gained in fulfilment and happiness had they dared to speak up and ask for what they wanted.

The price of disempowerment

Lincoln, 51, wanted to talk to his ex-wife about the many issues that remained unresolved when their marriage ended—including all their joint financial assets. But his memories of the anger and disdain that she had shown towards him throughout their relationship prevented him from saying what he needed to say. In his 18 years of married life with Julie, he had never really got what he wanted, or said what he needed to say, for fear of her reactions.

After the divorce, he felt a strong need to express all the issues that had come between them, but his fears stopped him short. His ex-wife held onto her anger, and all the grief associated with having never been able to reach her husband emotionally. She also held onto the house and all their joint possessions. Though financially comfortable, she had too much pain and anger in her heart to enjoy it.

For Lincoln, staying quiet was a lose-lose option.

How might things have been different if he had dared to express his feelings to his wife?

power—head on. We may even be truly convinced that there is no point in trying to be powerful because it will surely end in defeat. Yet it is only in our minds that others are powerful. In reality, they are no more so than we are, and it is only our skewed perception of them that makes them so. It is that easy for us to give our power away, and we do it without realizing what is at stake.

The balance of power

Every relationship is precious in terms of what it can teach us and how it provides us with an opportunity to express our love and personal power. Whether consciously or unconsciously, both partners come together to heal and become empowered as individuals. That is the fundamental purpose of their relationship, and the reason they came together. If the necessary healing takes place, then being in that particular relationship will have provided them with a very essential part of their personal-power puzzle.

In every relationship, there is usually one partner who has slightly greater awareness than the other, or who cares a little more—and just enough—to want to resolve things when they go wrong.

The partner with the greater awareness or willingness often has a natural desire to apply that knowledge in their relationship. It is no accident that they have acquired such awareness, and their desire for change or resolution is there for a reason. When wisely and lovingly applied, knowledge and desire can transform a dysfunctional relationship into a mind-blowing exploration of the deepest intimacy and sensuality available to humans. Failing to grasp precious opportunities for mutual growth and fulfillment can result in emotional separation, with both partners locked away in their private prisons.

In failing to embrace our power, we can become like human icebergs, with only the merest tip of our being showing above the surface, while the greater part of us remains submerged, with its vast, unfathomable beauty invisible even to ourselves.

If the potential for healing in a specific relationship is not fulfilled, and partners do not express their personal power on the many levels of expression available to them, they will carry the same issues with them into the next relationship. And, unless healing happens in between, the next relationship will necessarily be more traumatic and more painful so that the issues (now even more deeply entrenched and hardened over with past resentments and disappointments) can be brought back up to the surface for healing.

It is simple, once you really get it. Relationships are designed to make you whole. That is their primary purpose. They are there for you to explore and develop your personal power, and they come to you in very specific packages, perfectly tailored to your needs of the moment.

It is simple, once you really get it. Relationships are designed to make you whole. That is their primary purpose. They are there for you to explore and develop your personal power, and they come to you in very specific packages, perfectly tailored to your needs of the moment.

Imagine, then, the futility and self-defeat (not to mention the unnecessary pain) of not using relationships for their true purpose. Rebelling against them, or lashing out at a partner who seems to do nothing but trigger your pain, merely prolongs an inevitable process. At the simplest level, it means you are not yet ready to embrace the incredible power that resides inside you. And there is nothing wrong with that; there is a perfect time for this to happen for everyone.

But when you can turn to your partner and say, *"Let's go for it, no matter what. I'm ready to do whatever it takes to get to the naked, raw, scary love that I know is there inside me, somewhere"*, then you are saying *"yes"* to a power that has the entire universal network of opportunities, synchronicities, 'happy accidents', and miracles at its disposal.

Powerful on purpose

Every individual has a purpose, and it is normally through the fulfilment of this purpose that one expresses one's individual power. If you embrace that purpose, you will have a very specific effect on your world. If you avoid that purpose, then a totally different chain of events will ensue as a result.

A far-reaching domino effect results from your ability or failure to embrace your power and put it to its intended use—no matter how seemingly insignificant. If, for example, you were not confident enough to pull off that interview, then someone else got the job and you did not. Likewise, if you were powerful enough to get what you wanted, then someone else would be without that job and you would have it. Their life would follow a different course as a result, and so would yours. The ripples that radiate out from your action or inaction go further than you could ever imagine. Consider, then, how you are controlling more than your own small world, by virtue of the power you wield—purposely or passively.

But fulfilling one's purpose is not necessarily a matter of achieving one particular objective, such as becoming an opera singer or being a nurse. It is our unique path in life, along which we express our unique qualities, and strive to be all that we can be, while affecting all of those we meet along the way. If we want to fully express our power, we walk this path with a sense of purpose, aware of, and alert to, the signposts that direct us to the next stage of our particular journey and keep us on track. For personal power, like any other source of energy (be it electricity, wind or water) is part of a bigger whole. It has a source and, since everyone else has access to this same power, we are all connected through that same source. We can tap into it; we can draw from it. And, when we do, we are operating as part of a system—a vast, complex orchestration of interacting elements that work together in ways far beyond our understanding.

Because we are part of this energy network, or grid, every action we take, and even the thoughts we have, exert an influence on the whole. We cannot hide behind a veil of isolation, because what we do matters. It counts. It has an effect, whether we like it or not.

If we lose our way along our particular path, our body (our medium of powerful expression) will let us know. Ill-health, unhappiness, dissatisfaction, excess weight and depression can be some of the symptoms of power gone astray.

The power of sex

Sex is perhaps the most abused source of power on earth. Throughout the ages, it has been used as a weapon, a form of torture, a means of survival, a form of manipulation and control, an escape from painful issues or an empty life, a form of non-verbal power struggle, a substitute for commitment, a form of emotional and psychological abuse, and an expression of love.

Rarely, however, is it used for its intended higher purpose—spiritual union with a loved one, leading to a spiritual experience of love at the highest level.

In its purest form, sex is energy. And this energy is generated in the reproductive/creative centre of the body, between the belly button and the pubic bone. This area corresponds to the second chakra, or energy centre, which is also an important centre of power. It is here that our creativity is generated and many of our sensual and sexual responses occur.

But if the power of this energy centre is blocked or suppressed, it will express itself in other ways. It may take the form of fear (expressed as aggression or withdrawal), trauma (expressed as emotional dysfunction), or physical imbalance (manifesting as ill-health or weight problems).

When such issues remain unresolved, the sexual arena can turn into a battleground, with issues of intimacy and trust being the main weapons of choice. There is nothing more destructive in a relationship than unresolved pain that is projected by one partner onto another. And there is nothing that generates greater intimacy between two people than the healing of deep wounds together, because the love is huge when there are no barriers to what is inside the heart—including the pain. The deeper the wound that is healed, the more profound the intimacy that results.

There is nothing that generates greater intimacy between two people than the healing of deep wounds together.

Paying for a powerless past

David had had many disappointments in his past, and his ex-wife had spent most of their 20 years of marriage telling him how worthless he was and how he would never amount to anything. As a result, David had stored huge self-doubts, anger and resentment inside, and these deeply buried emotions were triggered whenever things went wrong.

His partner, Sue, was traumatized each time this happened, and nothing she said or did made any difference when David was 'lost' to his past. She could not reach him or reason with him during his outbursts because he was no longer present. As a result, Sue became aware of several 'no-go' zones in her relationship with David that made her very uneasy—sensitive topics that might spark another of his outbursts. This meant that she could not be totally herself with him, or feel totally free and relaxed.

For her part, Sue had had a history of emotional abuse, so David's violent outbursts made her withdraw to safety—both physically and emotionally. Intimacy was impossible given her fears of another outburst, and she did not feel safe enough to be sexually vulnerable with him. This, in turn, made David feel even more angry and frustrated. Like so many times before, he felt worthless in the eyes of his partner.

And so the cycle continued, growing in intensity as it did. Ironically, David was doing to Sue exactly what had been done to him by others before—making her feel worthless by treating her with disdain and disrespect.

With time, and with a growing awareness of her own issues, Sue came to realize that her part of the cycle was based on an old pattern of 'love at any cost'. She was so much in need of love that she experienced a huge sense of relief and a heart-flooding warmth each time David 'returned' from his angry wrestling match with his past and was his usual loving self. Initially, this had felt good—even sexually arousing—as the emotions were very intense and both partners were in need of love to heal their most recent wounds.

But Sue realized that this cycle was dysfunctional and that it was getting in the way of a deeper intimacy. She knew that, as with all abusive relationships, it would happen again and again until something radical was done to break the cycle. If left unresolved, she knew it would destroy their relationship and they would both walk away even more wounded than before.

Both partners needed to heal themselves by filling in their missing pieces and taking responsibility for their words and actions in the moment.

To break the power-struggle cycle, Sue needed to say "no" to the abuse from David and to refuse to be the dumping ground for any more refuse from his past. And David needed to acknowledge that he could not blame his ex-wife or his current partner for his problems. He had to take back responsibility for his emotions and for the dynamics in his life.

When two people are locked into the power struggle brought about by unresolved emotional pain, they create a cycle that is self-perpetuating. When the partner in pain lashes out at the other person, there can be a loss of respect, trust, safety and affection. (See 'Paying for a powerless past', opposite.)

But reclaiming one's power can be a deceptive process, if not done consciously and with an acute awareness of what is motivating it. If, for example, someone has been controlled for much of their life, and told what to do, they will want to regain control over their choices and be free to do what they want. However, in reaction to the control of the past, they may initially find themselves resisting any form of input in the present—however positive—even if doing so might ultimately prevent them from getting what they want.

Being powerful requires being present, but also mature and aware enough to know the consequences of your choices and the motivating forces behind them. Being present requires resolving issues from the past so that they no longer influence your choices or decisions in the present moment. Not surprisingly, it is the very process of resolving those issues that builds power and strength within the individual.

Power unplugged

Without connection, there is no power—at least, not the kind that moves mountains. If we do not connect with ourselves, we cannot access the power within us, nor can we connect with others or with the universe in general. We must connect at the deepest level in order to be powerful. When we are in touch with our deeper selves—with the love, the emotions, the dreams and the talents that make us uniquely us—we can connect with others at that same level. It is our emotions, our gifts and our dreams that connect us to the source of our power—like the wiring in a house or the nervous system in our bodies. Our emotions and our yearnings for fulfillment create a powerful charge that gets

connection

Connecting with our deeper selves and with those around us is the key to reclaiming and activating our power.

Connecting means using our:

- *words to penetrate, move, inspire and heal hearts, including our own;*
- *arms to reach out and embrace life, love and those close to us;*
- *eyes to explore and connect with nature, our neighbour, our loved ones and ourselves;*
- *limbs to transport us to new and daring places, to envelop others in love, and to connect with our partner physically in the act of sexual, spiritual union;*
- *sensitivity to caress, to understand and to experience compassion; and*
- *highly evolved minds to resolve problems, recognize our weaknesses, acknowledge our strengths, and defeat our fearful egos in the pursuit of our undeniable greatness.*

All of these aspects of our being are specifically designed for us to connect with self and others in the expression of our personal power. Avoiding eye contact, avoiding saying 'I love you', avoiding a kind gesture, or avoiding self-exploration is a denial of that unique expression.

transmitted to our body's fuse box (our brains) and to our transformer (our hearts). It is entirely up to us whether we blow our circuits by not allowing that charge to be expressed or by squandering the energy in other ways, or whether we block the transformation that can take place in our hearts, converting the powerful surge of energy into a manifestation of our desires. The power is there for us to use or abuse, and it is there for a reason.

When a partner fails to claim his or her own power, a vacuum is created. This is inevitably filled by the other partner, usually causing resentment on the part of the 'powerless' one, despite that person's failure to take charge. Ironically, those who are destined to become particularly powerful are often challenged by disempowering or controlling parents, teachers, bosses or partners.

In fact, the kind of partner that you attract can be a good indication of your major issues and challenges in life. If you have a controlling partner, for example, you are probably being called upon to find your power and put it to its intended use. If you attract abusive partners, it is highly likely that you need to work on building your self-esteem and self-worth, and to put those qualities to work for yourself in your life; and if you attract lacklustre relationships in which there is little or no passion, you are undoubtedly being prompted to get back in touch with your heart and what matters to you in life.

Relationships will always reflect back to you any aspects of your personal power that you are failing to embrace.

Power failures

When someone fails to embrace their power, it can be felt in very tangible ways by those involved.

A client of mine reported being extremely frustrated by a colleague who was consistently hesitant and unsure of himself at work. "I wanted to grab him by the shoulders and shake him till I got some kind of assertive reaction," she said. "He knew his stuff but he was so nervous and lacking in self-confidence that I found it physically draining to be around him. It affected everyone on the team. If he'd been able to rise to the challenge and share his ideas with us, I'm sure we would all have benefited. Instead, we all lost out."

Another client reported having a manager who consistently sidestepped his responsibilities and delegated important decisions to his staff. Although the manager had considerable authority, his personal fears caused him to mistrust his own judgement. He postponed making decisions for as long as possible and relied heavily on his staff for advice. As a result, he quickly lost the respect and credibility of his staff, whom he often unjustly blamed when things went wrong.

When we fail to be powerful, others often resent our insipidness because they know that a vacuum is being created and someone else will have to pick up the slack.

Avoiding potential pitfalls

- ***Don't give away your power.*** *It can only be taken from you if you allow it to be. If you do allow it, you assume the role of victim, which defeats the whole purpose of you being alive. You are here to be powerful in your own unique way.*
- ***Don't be afraid of your power*** *...unless you do not mind reaching old age, having achieved nothing and having never dared to be all that you could be. A positive expression of your power will always be well received. It is up to you to decide what form it takes and how great its impact.*
- ***Don't abuse your power.*** *Using your power to manipulate or control others not only destroys your relationships but also prevents that energy from being used to create something positive. Abusing one's power is the coward's way of being powerful because it is designed to disempower those around you who might otherwise pose a threat. True personal power is love put to good use, in whatever form.*
- ***Don't be stingy.*** *Being stingy with your personal power not only diminishes you but also deprives you of the opportunity to inspire or empower others to do something daring. Your power is a gift, designed to influence your world, so try not to keep it all to yourself.*

Chapter 13

Subtexts: reading between the lines

Some unspoken words are an eloquent betrayal of the truth.

How often have you said one thing but meant another? And how often do you react with anger and resentment when what you are feeling underneath is the pain of rejection?

We rarely say what we really mean, and we often do not dare to ask for what we really want. Unless we are solid and complete within ourselves, we tend to edit or censor our words in order to mask our true feelings and protect ourselves from possible pain or attack. We hide our vulnerability and any weakness we may associate with having been hurt, not heard or unappreciated.

Understanding the 'subtexts', or the true and deeper meaning behind another's words, provides us with a tool for resolving conflicts and generating productive, fulfilling relationships. The subtexts can indicate not only what another person is missing and therefore asking for, but also what is missing in ourselves, as reflected back to us by the words of others.

Jim, 26, worked as an architect for a large firm. Extremely hard working, he was being considered for promotion after only 18 months on the job. However, he was beginning to have problems with one of his colleagues—Sean—an older man who had not managed to move up the corporate ladder as fast as Jim. Although Jim did his best to be pleasant to Sean, he found the older man to be sarcastic and moody. Whenever Jim landed a contract, Sean would find some reason to criticize his work. Jim began to realize that there was more to Sean's words than met the eye. He began to look beneath what Sean was saying, and saw that his colleague's insecurity came from a lack of acknowledgement and recognition for his work. He recognized these elements as he himself had worked hard to create them in his own life, having missed them growing up. He knew that, because he worked closely with Sean, he was likely to have the same 'missing pieces' as his colleague. The absence of validation or recognition between them indicated that it was lacking on both sides. (Although Jim had managed to achieve some recognition in his job by working so hard, he received little validation in his personal relationships.)

To resolve the conflict, Jim began to acknowledge and praise Sean for his work. He looked for opportunities to genuinely compliment him, going out of his way to acknowledge him whenever he got a contract. At first, Sean was his usual sarcastic self, dismissing all Jim's attempts to be nice. However, after two months of consistent acknowledgment of Sean, Jim saw a change. Sean began to relax and respond without the sarcasm. He thanked Jim whenever he complimented him, and he even began to return the compliments, though somewhat gruffly at first.

Jim realized that Sean's life must have been so lacking in validation that it had required several months of coaxing and reinforcement to convince him that he deserved it. Only someone who was capable of understanding and reading Sean's subtexts would have persevered long enough to get to the truth beneath. In the process, Jim realized that his own need for recognition was one of the reasons he felt so driven in his work. He, too, began to relax, grateful that Sean had shown him one of his own 'missing pieces' and given him the opportunity to practise it. Jim had given Sean the gifts of acceptance and recognition, while giving himself the gift of a mutually-supportive, pleasant working environment. By having these missing qualities highlighted for him through Sean, he realized that validation was also missing in his relationship with his girlfriend and that he had the ability to make significant positive changes with her also.

When we are challenged with criticism or aggression of any kind, it can be difficult to respond with compassion and understanding. However, if we remind ourselves of the value of such incidents in our lives, and their function in showing us where the real source of the problem lies, then we can refocus and adjust our response to one of higher purpose. We can turn those unpleasant situations into opportunities for growth and healing in both directions. And, in doing so, we can generate what we want by providing what is needed to restore harmony and compassion.

We can turn unpleasant situations into opportunities for growth and healing.

Subtexts and how we miss out

Jenny says: *"Anna, I gather you can't make it this evening. No problem. I'll go on my own."*

What she really wants to say: *"That's the third time you've backed out of our arrangement. Ever since you got into that relationship you've had no time for me. I was useful enough when you were single, but now you obviously have better things to do."*

Here is a missed opportunity for any growing resentments to be nipped in the bud and resolved.

It could have gone like this:

Jenny: *"Anna, I feel you don't have time for me any more. I hardly ever see you now that you're with Steven. Isn't our friendship important to you?"*

Anna: *"Jenny, of course it's important to me. I'd be lost without your support. I'm so sorry you thought I was neglecting you. It's just that Steve and I have been having problems and I was afraid I'd be bad company. So I thought it would be better if I stayed at home and tried to sort it out by myself. Steve isn't even here. He's away for the weekend, so I can still come if you're sure I won't bore you to tears..."*

Jenny: *"For God's sake, come! You need to get out, and what are friends for, if not to listen to you moan about your problems?! We can talk about it and then go to see a funny movie or something to take your mind off it. How does that sound?"*

Now there is room for respect and more honest communication, even though it may not always be 'nice'.

Michael says: *"Yes, okay, I'll do it."*

What he really wants to say: *"I'm tired of always running errands for you, of always being expected to take care of you and the kids. What about me? Don't you ever think of doing those things for me? I never get time for myself."*

Here is a missed opportunity to generate closeness through mutual consideration and awareness.

It could have gone like this:

Michael says: *"Fiona, I feel worn out. I work all day, then I come home and have to fix the lawnmower, and help the kids with their homework. I feel there is nothing left for me or us. I miss having time alone with you. That never seems to happen these days. How can we get that back?"*

Fiona says: *"Sorry, love. I didn't realize you were tired. I'm exhausted too, but you always seem to have so much more energy than me, so I let you take charge. I just didn't think. You should have said something sooner..."*

Now there is room for negotiation and forgiveness. If both parties are willing, they can also agree to work on their respective issues of responsibility and consideration, finding practical ways to demonstrate these qualities to each other.

Jane says: *"Not tonight, I've got a headache."*

What she really wants to say: *"You haven't even noticed my new haircut, or asked me how my day went. And you expect me to jump into bed with you and be all amorous. All you ever think about is sex."*

Barry says: *"You've always got a headache. Why don't you take a pill or something? And why do I always feel as if it's my fault?"*

Here is a missed opportunity for the deeper intimacy that could result from honestly sharing the hurt, and from understanding her partner's real reason for not noticing her.

It could have gone like this:

Jane says: *"Sweetheart, I'm feeling hurt. You didn't notice that I got my hair cut. I was hoping you would like it but you didn't even comment. I feel that you don't even see me when you make love to me."*

Barry says: *"Honey, I'm so sorry. I'm stressed at work and worried sick about all our bills. I didn't want to say anything about your hair because I knew I would ask how much it cost, and I was afraid I'd get angry and spoil the evening. So I thought I could just make love to you instead, and hope that you would understand the stress I was under. Making love to you is the only thing that keeps me sane…"*

Jane says: *"But it didn't cost anything. Marianne did it for me at her house. You should know me better than that. I know we have money problems and I wouldn't go spending money on a haircut at the moment... I do understand the stress you are under."*

Now there is room for mutual love and understanding, instead of the added stress and resentments that would have come from covering up the subtext with a brush-off.

Speaking honestly can either enhance an already strong and mutually-supportive relationship or end one that is neither of these things.

Either way, the outcome is a positive one. Being honest can be the best way to ensure that we have nothing but supportive and loving friends around us. Playing the game of being nice often means we compromise our values and end up feeling resentful or being taken for granted. In being honest, we usually feel relieved as a result of saying what we felt, instead of carrying it around forever. If you have been hurt by something someone has said to you, it is best to honestly express that to the person concerned. This generates respect and appreciation on both sides, opening the way for a deeper, more meaningful relationship.

Ask yourself how many times in the day do you say what you truly mean. And how many times do you trot out a response on automatic pilot, not thinking about what you are really feeling? Every time your words belie your feelings, you are cheating yourself out of a fuller, richer, more rewarding experience. You are not being fully yourself, and you are perhaps missing out on a wonderful opportunity for intimacy, for connection, and even for greater success and fulfillment in your work or your personal life. You are, in fact, telling lies. And you are probably lying as much to yourself as to the person you are talking to.

When your words are not congruent with your feelings, internal conflict results. Your body and mind may be pulling you in one direction, but your words are taking you in another. This results in mixed messages being sent out from your electromagnetic field. One part says "yes", the other "no". One part wants to go forward, the other wants to go back. The confusion in your messages can result in confusion in your life, and you may wonder why you are feeling stuck or things are not happening as fast as you would like them to. When, on the other hand, your words are congruent with your feelings and your actions, they can be extremely powerful in producing a positive response.

If you feel uneasy at the thought of expressing an honest emotion, know this: the degree of uneasiness is commensurate with the effect that saying it would have on the person involved. In other words, the more 'charge' you feel behind what you truly want to say, the more powerful it will be. Of course, it is important to express things in a healthy way, without violence or malicious intent. But if you can honestly express yourself with respect, compassion and integrity, there is nothing more liberating or powerful.

As holistic beings, with everything rolled into one body—emotions, thoughts, beliefs, judgements, desires, dreams, movement, action—we are designed to operate as a collective whole, with each part complementing the other, not working against it. The very word individual means 'not to divide' (*in*, meaning 'not', and *dividere*, 'to divide'). If we negate our feelings with our words, we sell ourselves short and compromise our integrity.

Every time our words belie our feelings, we are cheating ourselves out of a fuller, more rewarding experience.

If we negate our feelings with our words, we sell ourselves short and compromise our integrity.

integrity

The word 'integrity' comes from 'integer', meaning 'a whole number'. And that is what we are—whole, a complete unit. When the heart speaks, the lips are meant to follow suit with the appropriate translation, speaking for the good of the 'unit'. Anything less is a betrayal, bound to lead to some kind of internal 'mutiny'.

Practising integrity means:

- *making a commitment to yourself to speak honestly, openly and from the heart to everyone you meet or communicate with. Notice how you feel when you are about to give your usual replies ("Yes, I'm fine, thank you", or "No, I don't mind doing that...")—if, in fact, you are feeling the very opposite;*
- *daring to stand behind your values, particularly in the face of a potentially negative reaction, and to express what you really believe in; and*
- *having the courage to express your feelings, even if doing so makes you feel vulnerable.*

Observe what happens. By practising integrity, you not only validate your feelings, but you also inspire others to do the same. Integrity is always a win-win option.

Avoiding potential pitfalls

- ***Don't try to pretend to be something you are not.*** *Dare to say what you mean and mean what you say.*
- ***Don't compromise yourself.*** *You have a unique perspective on life and your feelings and thoughts matter. Give others the gift of your authentic self and trust that that is what you are meant to do.*
- ***Don't cover up your hurt or feelings for the sake of others.*** *Maybe your feelings are just what they need in order to open their hearts or see something from a different perspective.*

Chapter 14

Parental payback: our emotional weaponry

There is no revenge as complete as forgiveness.

—Josh Billin

Some of us were fortunate to have had loving, affectionate, emotionally-balanced parents. Others had loving parents who just did not know how to show their love. And yet others had parents who were neglectful, thoughtless or downright abusive. But all of us had parents who were simply human and fallible, even though we expected them to be perfect.

It is the imperfections of our parents that we can sometimes interpret as personal slights, not understanding (as children) that our parents had their own challenges, fears, self-doubts or emotional trauma and perhaps needed love just as much as we did.

If our most fundamental needs (such as our need for love and nurturing) are not met in childhood, we may develop poor self-worth and a lack of belief in self. As a result, we can end up fulfilling our parents' subconscious fears about themselves (which get passed on to us in the form of their missing pieces). In doing so, we can make ourselves failures in life. Although rarely intended as such, this is the ultimate revenge against parents; as a product and reflection of them, our failures show them their own worthlessness. In the process, however, we can destroy our own lives.

Only by gaining a deeper understanding of our purpose and allowing ourselves to have the rewards of success (rather than the empty victory of revenge), can we discover the gift we hold for our parents, and the reason they gave birth to us in the first place.

When we have love-deprived parents, it means we have chosen no small challenge. The hardest thing to do on this planet is to love in the face of lovelessness. Yet, as sons and daughters, that is what our parents may most want and need us to do. We are our parents' gift to themselves. For how else can they find love in their life if no one close to them learns it and gives it back to them? It is often only the bond of the blood ties that keeps people around long enough to see through the surface layers covering up love. As children, we do not have the emotional maturity to understand that our parents' poor self-worth may come from a lack of love in their early years. Often it is only on their deathbed or in some emotional crisis that we get to see that our parents are really just insecure, love-deprived children trying to

Reproducing worthlessness

Al's mother was so deprived of love, validation and any sense of control over her life that she was convinced she was a victim of others. The only way she could have any feeling of self-worth was to blame everyone else for the misery of her life. Being a victim was a way of not acknowledging that the wretchedness of her life was of her own making, and it also enabled her to avoid acknowledging just how very wretched her life was.

If she had objectively asked herself what kind of person would speak, act or think the way she did, she would have come to some rather horrendous conclusions about how unworthy and unlovable she perceived herself to be. The only way for her not to look at that and to keep the grief, anger and despair tightly contained was to project her huge dissatisfaction with herself onto those closest to her. She did this most effectively with her son.

Al was a manifestation of her perceived worthlessness and a confirmation of what she had been taught about life. She had passed on to him her missing pieces of validation and love. Not surprisingly, Al was challenged in these same areas—his marriage fell apart, he could not find decent work, and he had grown negative, lazy and bitter about himself. His subconscious anger at his mother had caused him to opt out of life, and to become a disempowered victim himself. Without self-love and self-validation, he was unable to counter her negative beliefs and embrace his true potential.

behave like adults. If the child in them never got loved and nurtured, and could therefore never grow up, their behaviour can often seem childish, petty and vindictive.

When people do not have love reflected back to them, they may not even know that they lack love in their life. How can they miss what they have no conception of? Whatever is in their heart is their translation of love. Sometimes the reason for having children may be a lack of love in a relationship. Loveless couples may hope that having a child will bring them closer together. This would be true if they allowed the child's innate wisdom of love and trust to flow over them and fill them up. But if parents lack those qualities themselves, it can be difficult for them to allow such things in, and so they often end up crushing the very qualities they had hoped to give birth to.

The hardest thing to do on this planet is to love in the face of lovelessness.

As a son or daughter, you can choose to see yourself in several ways—as a victim of your mother or father, which would place her or him in a position of power over you, or as a huge gift to your mother, for example. Perhaps she gave birth to you so that you would love her back to life.

As children, we are brimming over with love, but it can quickly become suppressed and conditional if our own basic needs are not met. The love is still in there, nonetheless, and offering it up in the face of lovelessness just may be the most powerful, scariest and noblest thing you ever do in your life.

We may think that our parents owe us and we may expect them to be wise, healthy, balanced and... well, perfect. Because that is how we know ourselves to be. We know, deep down, that that is our true essence, so it is not just a shock to know that our parents are not everything we thought they should be; it is also a shock to be told that, by extension, we are not perfect, either.

The wonderful, magical thing about healing our own wounds is that that our healing radiates out in waves to those around us.

The wonderful, magical thing about healing our own wounds is that that our healing radiates out in waves to those around us. When we break our own part of the cycle, we also break it for the other person involved. And when we learn to love ourselves enough to be powerful, successful and loved, then the impact of that love flows back to our parents because, as a product of them, we show them that they have value and that they are worthy of the same success and love.

Once one family member starts to heal, the effect can be felt throughout the entire family, and there is no denying it. However, healing may take different forms for different people, at different times. Some may be irritated by another's success or loving relationship, and may do their utmost to reject its validity because it confirms the lack of such love or success in their own lives. And if they acknowledged that success and love were possible, they would have to make big changes—in their deeply entrenched beliefs about their own self-worth and the disappointments that they believe would surely result if they even attempted to get what they wanted out of life.

If some family members are too emotionally attached to their limiting beliefs and refuse to contemplate the possibility of a better life, they may even reject the person who has found love, success, etc. A family argument may ensue, leading to a distancing of the 'catalyst' so that the safe wall of denial may be maintained.

Others may want positive change, and may put a tentative toe in the water to test the temperature. But, without the conviction of their own worthiness, they may recoil at the first hint of disappointment or failure—even if such things are only a reflection of their current beliefs about themselves and, therefore, the inevitable starting point in the whole healing process.

But all these reactions take place because things have been stirred up and because people may not believe that the same positive transformations are also possible for them. For some, it can take time to let good things in, and lasting happiness may not be something they can conceive of ever having. Others, whose hearts may be a bit more open, may be inspired to make changes in their own lives and to embark upon their own healing journey.

I have seen how love can heal an entire family, and it is a wonderful phenomenon to witness. The family represents our initial and most immediate sphere of influence in the world, and it is here that we often first get to practise loving in the face of lovenessness, giving in the face of nothing given, or succeeding in the face of unrelenting negativity. If we can do this, we can go forth into the larger world of relationships, community, and even entire societies to make our loving presence felt and to help heal the world in our own unique way.

Avoiding potential pitfalls

- ***Don't blame your parents.*** *They almost certainly had unmet needs and you may be one of the few people who can recognize and give them what they have been missing all their lives. (If abuse has been an issue, you may need to address this with them, no matter how painful it may be, in order to reclaim yourself.)*
- ***Don't be deterred by family dynamics that get on your nerves.*** *Remember that it only takes one to break the cycle and you can refuse to play the same old family games.*
- ***Don't try to change your family or have any expectations of them.*** *They will change (or not) at their own pace, and all you can do is make positive changes for yourself and hope that they benefit too.*
- ***Don't limit your view of your parents to being only that—parents.*** *They are also human beings and, if you relate to them as a friend rather than their child, there is room for more positive, loving dynamics to emerge.*

Part IV

Growing and evolving in our relationships; troubleshooting techniques to help prevent us from falling back into old patterns and beliefs

Chapter 15

Going deeper

One of the most important ways to make love work for you in your relationships is learning how to communicate the complete truth.
—Barbara de Angelis

Intimacy has many forms and, in a committed, loving relationship, the possibilities for creating ever-deeper intimacy are infinite. But going deeper with a partner often brings up fears, insecurities and self-doubts. And, unless we are acutely aware of what our fears or doubts represent, we can subconsciously push intimacy away by creating its opposite—separation and distance.

Starting arguments, cracking jokes, getting drunk, and doing or saying hurtful things are just some of the creative strategies we can use to keep intimacy at bay.

As with many other relationship issues, intimacy depends on close communication and connection with yourself and with your partner. Without this, true intimacy cannot develop. There may be great sex, but there will be no intimacy unless the emotional barriers are removed. By agreeing to adopt some simple communication tools, you can create a safe and open forum for the spontaneous expression of your fears, self-doubts and desires, which might otherwise remain unspoken. Expressing your deepest feelings in this way is, in itself, a very intimate process, with the power to open hearts, heal wounds and take you deeper into yourself and your relationship.

Clearing the way to better communication

No matter how much work we might do on ourselves or our relationships, there will always be times when tempers flare, fatigue clouds our judgement or we're just too upset, hurt or emotional to care about doing or saying the 'right' thing to our partner. And that's okay. Getting 'fit for love' is not about becoming a saint or creating a relationship that never has any challenging moments; as pathways to personal empowerment, relationships are designed to present us with opportunities for growth.

Sometimes it is good and healthy to express hurts and grievances and to just let them rip in the heat of the moment. If we are in a committed, conscious relationship, it may be safe to do this if our partner is aware that we are merely venting and does not take it personally. Sometimes, however, this is hard to do and our partner may react to our outburst with one of his/her own. Things can then spiral down into angry, hurtful exchanges and resentment, which can end with an impasse. When this happens, the following communication tool can be used to help resolve it.

Agree to take time out from the angry exchange and go to separate rooms to cool off. Use this time to examine your part in the conflict, reminding yourself that you created this situation with your partner and that you put him or her there so that he or she could trigger your issues and show you what is missing inside yourself. It might feel as if he or she is to blame for this, but if you have done the work of the preceding chapters, you will know that there is more to it than that.

See the boxes below and overleaf for an example of how you can objectively assess your part in the conflict and what you can do to resolve it.

The argument

Kate and Julian were both very committed to their relationship and to working through their personal issues. But one persistent problem seemed to be completely beyond their ability to resolve it: Julian snored almost every night and Kate could not sleep. They had argued over this countless times, with Kate suggesting dietary changes and weight loss, and Julian telling her that she was too light a sleeper and should figure out how to sleep more deeply. Neither wanted to sleep alone, but it was starting to look as if that was the only option left.

They awoke one morning after a particularly disturbed night. Julian had snored all night long and Kate had been woken repeatedly. She had only managed to get about three hours' sleep and was resentful and exhausted when she got up.

"Are you okay?" Julian asked her over breakfast.

"No, I'm not," Kate replied. "I hardly slept because of your snoring."

Julian goes quiet.

"I don't see why I should feel bad about this," Kate said. "I'm sick of wearing ear plugs and having to block out the noise. It just doesn't work."

"Oh, so it's my fault again. I can't do anything right, can I. I try eating less, I drink less, I go on all sorts of diets, but it's never enough. I'm the one who's always wrong!"

"It's not about being wrong!" said Kate. "I just want to find a solution."

"Look, if you want to sleep alone, just say so."

"But I don't. I want to be able to sleep with you and to wake up rested, like you do."

"So what do you expect me to do about it? You want me to stop eating altogether? You'd be much better off sleeping on your own anyway. I'm just a big noisy, hairy nuisance at night."

"Oh for God's sake… I'm sick of this!"

Kate storms out of the room, too frustrated for words.

The resolution

Acknowledge that you have just been triggered and try to answer the following questions:

1. *What exactly are you angry/hurt/upset about and why?*
2. *What did your partner do/say that triggered this in you?*
3. *What might be the trigger or missing piece(s) in this scenario?*
4. *What can you take responsibility for?*
5. *How did you react to what he/she did or said?*
6. *How could you have responded differently?*
7. *What would you like to express to your partner now and how could you do that calmly, lovingly, consciously?*

For Kate, the answers went something like this:

1. *I'm furious at Julian for not understanding how hard this is for me and that there is nothing I can do to fix it. I feel misunderstood, not heard and abused.*
2. *He got angry without trying to find a solution or understand how I might feel after a sleepless night.*
3. *My trigger could be 'powerless' and my missing pieces 'consideration', 'respect' and 'intimacy'.*
4. *I chose him as my partner and I need to look at what he's showing me about myself, rather than blaming him. I could have chosen to sleep in the other room.*
5. *I reacted in an accusatory way and presented him with the same old problem without suggesting a new approach or asking for his help.*
6. *I could have asked him how he felt about it and if he could think of anything else that we could try. I could have tried to understand his frustration.*
7. *I would like to say I'm sorry for getting worked up and lashing out at him. I would like to hold him and tell him that I want to remove all my barriers to intimacy with him; I know that I created this because I still have some fears over getting too close.*

Julian's answers were a little different:

1. *I hate hurting Kate and I feel depressed when I upset her and don't know how to fix it.*
2. *She blamed me for the problem and made me feel wrong, just like my first wife always did. That took me right back to all those years of anger and frustration when I felt utterly powerless and rejected.*
3. *My trigger is probably 'unlovable' or 'worthless' and the missing pieces 'love', 'affection', 'support' and 'understanding'.*
4. *I could eat less before bedtime as I know I often snore when I go to sleep on a full stomach. I could offer to sleep in the other room a few nights a week until we resolve this.*
5. *I reacted by getting angry with Kate and then pushing her away with my words.*
6. *I could have listened and tried to understand her frustration at not being able to sleep. I could have been gentler and more considerate of her feelings.*
7. *I would like to explain that she triggered some old painful issues in me, which I want to resolve. I would like to tell her that I'm worried about money, which made me cranky and intolerant. I would like to take her in my arms and tell her that I love her.*

Now share your insights and feelings with your partner. Having recognized your part in creating the conflict, make a commitment to yourself to fill in your missing pieces in order to remove the barriers to greater intimacy.

Re-awakening the body

The process of going deeper with our partner can be enhanced on another, more sensual, level. Although we need touch in order to connect with others, there is a part of us that is rarely touched. It is just above the surface of our physical selves and we are totally unaware of it, most of the time. It is linked to our nervous system, and therefore to every part of us, every organ, every gland, every muscle. It is like a subtle second skin, an extension of our physical form and yet part of it. It is the layer of energy—the aura—that surrounds our body and it is constantly transmitting and receiving information. It is the interface between us and the outside world.

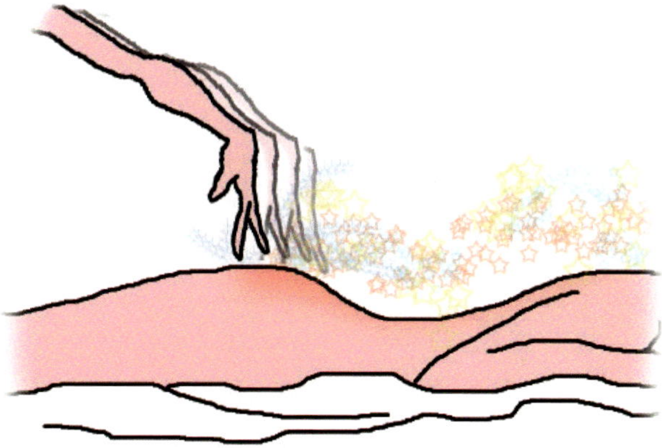

We cannot easily massage or stimulate our internal organs, but we can use this outer layer of energy to send messages to them and to bring them back to life if they have become congested, lethargic or numb.

By very delicately and slowly running the fingers or the palm of the hand over the surface of the skin, we can awaken and enliven the whole body via the central nervous system. With *aurage*—the sensory, sensual massage of the aura—we can reach parts deep inside us that have been asleep or that we never even knew existed. This technique is extremely powerful, and it can be used to heighten sensory awareness, help you get back in touch with your body, or enhance sexual pleasure in areas that you might not formerly have considered as erogenous zones.

It is also a powerful technique for couples to use if they have lost the edge to their love-making, or can no longer communicate their feelings adequately. Without the need for words, *aurage* speaks a body language all its own. It is the language of touch, expressed with delicate loving tenderness and sensuality. Even if there are no amorous or sensual feelings at the beginning of the process, the body soon comes to life, stimulated on many levels by the energy that is transmitted by the fingers to the nerves, creating powerful sensations throughout the body.

When *aurage* is properly done, slowly and with focus, the bodily and energetic sensations can be exquisite and may even help individuals to achieve orgasm or to greatly enhance their sexual experience. Because energy is being transmitted and sent charging through the body via the energy channels (or meridians), there is far greater bodily participation in the process, and love-making becomes an all-body experience, rather than being focused purely on the usual erogenous zones. When there is a loving connection between two individuals and when they take the time to caress each other in this way, *aurage* can elicit deep and intense feelings, bringing up deeply buried emotions or rekindling passion.

'Aurage' is an exquisite titillation of the senses that stimulates the body's sexual reflexes.

Most of all, though, it is an exquisite titillation of the senses, an explosion of sensory delight that stimulates the body's sexual reflexes.

Touching your way to ecstacy

Although you are essentially massaging the aura, you are actually touching the skin very lightly, brushing the fine hairs on the body to stimulate nerve endings. For the most powerful experience, it is best to start with the feet, which often turn out to be one of the most sensitive parts of the body. Moving from the toes slowly up the legs, inside and out, energy is drawn from the lower limbs up towards the torso. The genital area is avoided for the moment, and the focus is on drawing energy from the lower limbs towards the centre of the body. After moving from toes to calves, thighs and hips, move to the top of the head and begin to work downwards, towards the lower abdomen. The back is a particularly sensitive area with so many nerve endings along the spine, and this should be caressed before touching the front of the torso. Another important area is the base of the spine, between the buttocks and just above them. This is a storehouse of tremendous sexual energy (the second chakra, or energy centre, which relates to creativity, reproduction and sensitivity, is located here), and stimulating this area can often help to release blockages at the sexual, physical and energetic levels.

As the process continues, the sexual energy builds, and the focus is drawn to that all-important area where torso meets lower limbs. If the fingers circle the genital area like a wary predator, holding back from contact for as long as possible, then, when contact finally comes, the experience can be explosive.

While this process may often seem purely sexual in its outcome, there is a great deal more happening beneath the surface than may be apparent. The body is brought back to life on many levels, and once it has been stimulated and sensitized to touch (as the gateway to what is inside) it is important that it be followed by either very tender love-making or intimacy of some form (sharing or some form of communication). Intense feelings often create vulnerability, and the vulnerability that comes from opening up in this process provides a valuable opportunity for reconnecting—both with yourself and your partner. Take the time to explore this valuable opening and the opportunity it presents for generating greater intimacy in your relationship.

Avoiding potential pitfalls

- ***Don't mask your fears of intimacy with your usual tactics*** *(creating arguments, being flippant, or suddenly remembering that you have a huge pile of ironing to do). Pushing your partner away means you both lose out, whereas expressing your feelings opens up exciting new possibilities for shared, safe intimacy.*
- ***Don't prolong the agony.*** *If you are in a relationship for love and growth, then confronting scary intimate issues is an inevitable part of it. Don't postpone intimacy until some other 'perfect' time. It may never come and you will have missed an opportunity for deeper love and fulfillment. And if you are not in the relationship for love and growth, ask yourself why you are in it.*
- ***Don't let life get in the way.*** *We all have many seemingly 'legitimate' reasons for not wanting to get close—too much stress at work, too many errands to run, or not feeling well. These are all reasons for enhancing intimacy rather than avoiding it, since our partner may take great pleasure in giving us a relaxing massage, preparing a romantic meal, or otherwise showering us with tender loving care. Let it in and let it nourish you.*

Chapter 16

Meaningful marriage

A good marriage is one that allows for change and growth in the individuals and in the way they express their love.

—Pearl S. Buck

Marriage, in its truest sense, is the commitment to a journey. It is an agreement between two partners to explore life together, and to support and love each other in the process of healing wounds and becoming empowered as individuals.

Marriage does not necessarily need to be sanctioned by law or approved of by society. It is a private and very personal union that usually requires two basic elements: a desire to grow in love and a willingness to share.

Marriage, in this context, is considered to be any committed relationship between two people. If a couple wish to enter into a 'conscious' marriage or life together, they may choose to abandon many of the conventional rules, knowing that their marriage cannot be bound by static promises or predetermined timelines. Conscious marriage is an ongoing process of choice, sustained by open, honest communication. It is the freedom born out of daily choosing to be with your loved one—out of unconditional love, rather than need or dependence. And this kind of marriage is built on a mutual willingness to live with integrity, authenticity and self-respect. This is a commitment that involves growing, evolving, following your heart and being the best person that you can possibly be. If both partners do this, they will always be true to each other, even if that truth ultimately takes them on separate paths.

Ironically, as divorce has become easier to obtain and the institution of marriage has lost its former grip on society, marriage has become increasingly meaningful for many couples seeking a conscious relationship. Now, couples can freely choose to embark on something that they know they can equally freely get out of. It is within their control, and they can decide how, when and where it will be celebrated, and for how long it will last. As conscious individuals, they will also be aware that their relationship is their pathway to self-discovery, growth and wholeness.

Marriage muscle

The best marriages are built on flexibility and 'muscle'—and nowhere more so than in the heart.

Without emotional flexibility and strength, even the most loving couples can grow apart.

Building and maintaining this 'muscle' involves:

1. ***enriching the relationship** by continuing to grow and learn as an individual. In this way, you stay dynamic within yourself and keep your relationship alive. Without growth, you stagnate, and no meaningful marriage can withstand chronic stagnation. Boredom, routine and predictability are the biggest killers of relationships. Promoting and taking responsibility for your own growth is crucial to sustaining creativity and passion.*

2. ***staying healthy and fit.** Your body is your means of expression—your sensual, creative, individual expression. Keeping it healthy means that energy flows and organs are kept vital. And a healthy body is far more emotionally stable than an unhealthy one. It is a mark of respect for your partner to take care of yourself. Likewise, neglecting your body is a sign that love is lacking somewhere along the line, and that you no longer care enough to make an effort. It can be the first sign that you—and therefore your relationship—are on shaky ground.*

3. ***maintaining friendships outside the marriage.** This is vital to the life force of your marriage. Making your partner the centre of your universe puts a huge strain on the relationship and ultimately leads to isolation, an unhealthy focus on small things, and an ever-decreasing range of expression. No meaningful marriage can sustain itself in a universe of two.*

4. ***seeking greater awareness** of one's self and of one's partner. Understanding how you tick, what makes you reactive, and how to distinguish between your own issues and those of your partner is key to keeping your marriage healthy and clean. A 'clean' relationship is one that has no clutter—no buildup of resentments, no things left unsaid, no holding on to hurts, no grudges borne. Tackling issues in the moment is the only way to ensure that your marriage stays clean and your love strong.*

5. ***creating surprises.** Like any longstanding arrangement—be it marriage or a job—things can become lacklustre after a while. By going out of your way to create surprises for your loved one, you can avoid the deadly erosion of daily routine. Break from routine. Try something new. Surprise your partner with a gift, an outing, two tickets for a cruise. Use your imagination, be creative and you will probably find that it brings you even more pleasure than it does your partner.*

6. ***maintaining sexual 'tension'.** When a couple's sex life is alive and well, there is an 'elastic band' that naturally exists between them, connecting them and dynamically pulling them back to each other after healthy periods of separation. Going away on a course, regularly visiting family or taking a trip alone can help to maintain this sexual tension. Time spent alone can be all the richer for knowing that you will be returning to your partner. And spending time with your partner is all the more enjoyable after time spent alone. This is a natural cycle that conscious couples enjoy. If you experience distress or unhappiness when spending time away from your partner, this may indicate an unresolved need within yourself, or a missing element in your marriage that should probably be addressed.*

7. ***encouraging each other to take emotional risks and to go for what you want.*** *Supporting and encouraging your partner to take healthy risks is part of helping them to realize their fuller potential. You may feel threatened by your partner's growth, or by a move that could shift the dynamic between you, but (as a conscious partner) you will recognize the danger of trying to maintain the status quo and to remain within your comfort zone. Change is to be welcomed, because it helps to keep your marriage, and each of you, alive and dynamic. Staying small or stuck, or trying to keep your partner small, will ultimately suffocate your relationship.*

8. ***always expressing feelings in the moment.*** *This is especially important if something hurtful has been said or done. There is nothing that will cause a meaningful marriage to deteriorate faster than unspoken hurts or disappointments. Resentments build up and the heart shuts down. Love cannot flourish in these conditions, and intimacy loses its depth. Conversely, there is nothing that creates greater intimacy between two individuals than the heartfelt expression of their emotions.*

9. ***being able to say sorry.*** *Saying you're sorry often feels like an admission of failure or weakness. But being able to apologize to someone—sincerely, from the heart—is one of the most powerful things you can do in a relationship. It means that you are more interested in being happy than in being right, and that you are willing to rise above the need to make someone else wrong. And saying sorry does not necessarily mean that you are wrong. It may simply mean that you regret how you handled something or how your words or actions inadvertently hurt someone. It may mean that, even though you consider yourself to be right in what you say, you regret having made it an issue and are willing to look at another way of resolving it. Whether you are in the 'wrong' or not, saying sorry, when it is genuine, can make everything 'right'.*

10. ***saying "I love you" in novel ways.*** *The words "I love you" can cease to feel meaningful when they are repeated countless times over the years. Changing the context or the way in which you express your love helps to keep it meaningful. It may be through a poem, a painting, a special gift. It may be in a letter, sent in the mail to your partner, even if he/she lives with you. It may be in the way you caress or sensually appreciate your partner. It may be in the way you make love—without any words, or by focusing exclusively on your partner, not allowing him/her to touch you. Taking exceptional trouble over a birthday gift—such as organizing a treasure hunt, having a taxi arrive unexpectedly to take your partner to a secret venue—can be an exciting way of expressing your love. If you find yourself running out of ideas, look at your own life and see where you can inject new passion and sparkle. In a conscious marriage, where the embers of love are regularly stoked, the radiance of one partner illuminates the other.*

Finding novel ways to express your love helps to keep marriage meaningful.

Chapter 17

Using your unique gifts

If you have a talent, use it in every which way possible. Don't hoard it. Don't dole it out like a miser. Spend it lavishly like a millionaire intent on going broke.
—Brendan Francis

Exploring and expressing your individual uniqueness is the key to keeping your relationship—and your passion for life—alive.

Relationships can quickly grow stale if we stop growing. Unless we continue to evolve and to strive to be all that we can be, our relationship—with our self and with our partner—loses its dynamic edge, leading ultimately to the death of our passion.

We all have gifts or talents of some kind, but we often avoid accessing or using them because we do not believe that they will be appreciated or recognized by others. We may spend our entire lives secretly harbouring dreams that never get fulfilled, or we may dabble in a pastime or hobby that could, instead, be transformed into a lucrative livelihood that we love. We resist our own greatness because we lack faith in ourselves; and our self-doubt can lead us to believe that it is preferable to live with the dream rather than to put it to the test and risk failure—thereby killing the dream for good, and letting a part of us die in the process.

Using our gifts is usually not considered a matter of life or death. And this may well be the reason that many of us do not strive to be the best that we can be; unless pushed to do so, we often prefer to stay 'safe'. As humans, we are taught to endure the seemingly inevitable routine, drudgery and hardship of everyday living. We learn how to exist but few of us are taught how to thrive, even though that is our natural state.

Our belief in such inevitability can get in the way of our passion, and sometimes only tremendous anger, sadness or frustration is powerful enough to break through the numbness of endurance to prompt us to seek a fuller life. A meaningless job or a loveless relationship can trigger feelings of defeat or sadness, prompting us to 'do or die'. We may sense that there is more to life and, if there isn't, we may even decide that we want no part of it. 'Checking out' can seem like an attractive option when compared with a life of pain and emptiness. If we reach this point, the prospect of confronting our fears and doing something daring in life may, by comparison, seem far less daunting.

What would it take for you to activate your gifts and present them to the world? Would you need to be challenged by poverty, boredom, lack of fulfillment, loss of a limb or some other misadventure in order for you to attempt to be all that you could be? Would things be different if you knew you had only a year to live?

Those who have been seriously disadvantaged in life often achieve extraordinary things. For them, perhaps doing so *is* a matter of life and death. For if they have been deprived of sight or the ability to move, for example, they may need to compensate in other ways in order to survive, get the most out of life or retain their sanity—ways that often require super-human efforts on their part, or the heightened development of other senses or faculties. Disability and genius are not mutually exclusive—as individuals such as Stephen Hawking and Helen Keller have shown (see 'Defying the odds'). In fact, one may well be the direct result of the other.

The process of discovery

You may be aware of a gnawing inside you that is driving you to explore deeper parts of yourself and to get more out of life. If so, that's a good start. It is in embracing this exploration that you begin to embark upon the path of discovering and living your special gifts.

But to get more out of life, you must, not surprisingly, put more in. Do you know what you contribute to your world? And do you know what you are holding back? (You may be holding back certain emotions, in addition to certain talents that you have, and these are just as valid in helping you determine your special gifts.)

Cataloguing your emotional 'uppers' and 'downers' is a useful exercise to help you discover and assess your unique abilities and reveal what you can offer the world (see exercises 9–12 on pages 123–125). What makes you

Defying the odds

Born in 1880, Helen Keller became deaf and blind as a result of a childhood illness at the age of 19 months, and had only the faculty of touch with which to relate to the world. She had none of the reference points that most of us take for granted. She would not have been able to read this book, to appreciate colours, to see passion in a lover's eyes, to see her own face in a mirror, or to hear the laughter of a child. And yet she learned how to communicate through touch, she wrote and published several books, she campaigned for the deaf-blind, she travelled worldwide on lecture circuits, and she became the first deaf-blind person to earn a Bachelor of Arts degree. She had an extraordinary mind, and her ability to learn was far beyond anything before seen in someone without sight or hearing.

Was adversity the mother of excellence? Did her extra-ordinary challenges in life make her an extra-ordinary person? It is very likely that they did, for she had to apply her mind to learn techniques and aptitudes that most of us would find truly daunting, if placed in her shoes. With all her personal challenges, she did more than most of us will do in a lifetime of good health, with all our faculties intact.

> ### *Shopping for 'complements', and finding the perfect fit*
>
> *Julie had been a technical editor for 15 years. She was bored with her job and wanted to do something more creative. But, given her qualifications, she couldn't figure out what other options she had. So I asked her what she really loved doing. "Shopping," she said. What kind of shopping, I asked her. "Clothes shopping," she said, "but for the kind of clothes that really complement who I am, that reflect how I feel and are an expression of my personality."*
>
> *Julie discovered that she had a gift for finding the right colour, texture and style of clothing for women in all shapes and sizes, and it was something she loved doing. As we discussed the idea, she began to see how she could turn it into a very creative and rewarding business—taking clients on a shopping spree and finding the perfect clothes for them.*
>
> *Not only that, but she discovered that she had a knack for assessing her customers' desire for change, and would encourage them to try something totally different, to reflect the person they were striving to become—and to actually help them become that by enhancing their self-image.*
>
> *It can be that simple.*

feel good? What drains you, emotionally? What kind of people do you like to have around you? What inspires you? Is it politics or making wine? Is it cooking or weird and wonderful inventions? Is it music or making clothes? Whatever you really enjoy has the potential to be part of your unique life's work.

Finding out what makes you tick can help you determine your unique gifts. We tend to be good at things we enjoy doing, even if we require some training or practice as a beginner. Doing what we enjoy generates positive energy, whereas doing what we dislike has a negative effect—both on our energy levels and on the messages we transmit to our partners and the outside world. Positive energy nourishes us, opens doors for us and can take us to new and unexpected places. Negative energy, on the other hand, weighs us down, keeps us stuck and saps us of the motivation or drive to move forward.

If we can daily practise conscious choosing, authentic interaction and healthy acceptance of ourselves and others, we can come to an understanding and recognition of our unique contribution to the world.

Taking the plunge

There are three important ingredients that can help you to realize your unique potential and share your gift with others: faith, courage and inspiration.

Faith is not something that you develop as a result of logical analysis. Nor is it anything to do with religion. By definition, it is unquestioning belief and complete trust or confidence, without any tangible evidence to back it up. When you have faith in yourself and in your abilities, you can produce amazing results. But if you can extend your faith to include an acceptance of your undeniable place in the universe and your connection to a higher source of power, then you open yourself up to limitless possibilities.

Courage, unlike faith, is something you can muster. You can make yourself rise above your fears in order to do something that is important to you. You can use logical arguments to persuade yourself that it is worth taking a risk. And, of course, you can fill in any 'missing pieces' within yourself so as to be more open to success.

Inspiration feeds both faith and courage, making all things seem possible, even if our logical minds argue otherwise.

According to *Webster's New World Dictionary*, to inspire means 'to breathe in, to stimulate or impel as to some creative effort', and 'to motivate, as by divine influence'. From the same Latin root (*in spirare*), we also have the verb 'to inspirit', meaning 'to put spirit into'. Yet rarely do we think of our breath as being a source of inspiration or divine guidance.

As the word implies, inspiration is something that enters us from somewhere outside of ourselves—a force, an intuitive connection, a starburst of comprehension, transmitted to our hearts, our minds, or maybe even just our electromagnetic field.

The very act of breathing reminds us that our physical bodies play an important part in the process of being inspired. When we breathe in air (a combination of gases and molecules of myriad substances from our environment), we are connecting with something 'out there'. In fact, we are depending on something out there to keep us alive. Increasing our breathing (as in aerobic exercise), or slowing it down (as in the practice of yoga or meditation), has an impact at the physical, mental, emotional and spiritual levels. The former enlivens our bodies and stirs up emotions and energy that may give rise to ideas, and the latter connects us with a deeper part of ourselves and enables us to feel our connection with the rest of the universe. Doing both (having already done the work of the preceding chapters in this book)

Inspiration

Anything that generates an emotional reaction has the potential to inspire us. And it might not necessarily be a positive, happy feeling; any deep, heartfelt emotion has the potential to bring out the most authentic, raw, honest parts of us. I, for example, often do my best writing when I am angry or frustrated.

To help you get inspired:

- *shake up your body—through dance or any form of aerobic exercise;*
- *stimulate your emotions, using music, nature, art, writing or whatever gets you going;*
- *open yourself up to divine influence via meditation or yoga;*
- *discipline yourself by setting aside at least an hour every day to work on your ideas, or your gifts, if you already know what they are;*
- *seek feedback on your ideas from someone you trust to give you positive support and constructive criticism;*
- *have faith in your connection with the universe, and daily affirm your openness to receiving help from new and unexpected sources;*
- *be open, bearing in mind that your job is to be creative and proactive in the pursuit of your dreams, and not to figure out in advance how things will happen.*

You are free to choose: 'safe' routine or a life of daring adventure.

is a powerful way to enhance your creativity and get in touch with your gifts.

Many artists and musicians claim to have been overcome with creative surges that transported them to heights of rare excellence and beauty in their work. Some have claimed to be in direct communication with early masters, long since deceased. What is it that enables them to make this connection? And where did the early masters' inspiration originally come from? How did Leonardo da Vinci or Pythagoras, for instance, come up with concepts never before conceived of—concepts that have transformed the way we live and think?

If we can strengthen or enhance our connection with the source of this inspiration, then we may be able to use it more proactively in the application of our particular gifts.

Movement, dance, meditation, yoga, love or beauty are all potential means of inspiring ourselves; all involve getting in touch with a deeper part of ourselves and of opening up to divine influence.

Keeping the faith

Applying your gifts is a matter of faith. When you have filled in your main missing pieces, identified the things that perpetuate your cycles, and healed some wounds in your relationship (or ended an unhealthy one), you are ready to really make magic happen in your life. Faith is like the raising agent in a cake. Without it, everything falls flat. But when you mix it with inspired, courageous decisions, as well as positive action, intent and focus, you have all the ingredients for success. And when you bake a good cake, doesn't everyone normally want a slice?

Making it happen

- Focus on the activities you enjoy doing and visualize doing them (see Exercise 9).
- Imagine being helped from all quarters—by your friends, your family, acquaintances, networkers and the universe in general.
- Practise visualizing this scenario for 20 minutes every day for a month and allow yourself to consider the seemingly impossible.
- Affirm that you are open to receiving help and that you are ready to be successful in your dream venture.
- Focus on your main missing pieces and imagine yourself with those pieces filled in.
- See yourself as confident, safe, self-sufficient—whatever it would take for you to move forward.
- Do not allow your negative mind to interfere. This is your private dream time and it must remain untainted by any negativity or limitations.

By doing this daily, you will open yourself up to new and exciting possibilities. You must then be willing to let in the new and to acknowledge the fact that you had a part in making it happen.

Exercise 9

Make a list of your hobbies and any other activities that you enjoy. Then ask yourself what it is about those activities that feels good. Is it because you connect with other people or enjoy helping them? Is it because you get great satisfaction from making things with your hands? Or is it because you get completely absorbed and lose yourself in the experience?

Hobbies/activities that I enjoy	***Why they feel good***

Exercise 10

List the things you currently do in your life that do not feel good; ask yourself what it is about these activities that you do not like, and why you do them. Try to express your answer in terms of your feelings and possible 'missing pieces'. For example, if you are staying in your current job because you need the money, you may be afraid of letting go of the security provided by your job. Your missing piece might therefore be safety or healthy independence. Or it could relate to your self-worth and a belief that you do not deserve to succeed.

Activities I dislike doing	***Why I dislike doing them***	***I do them because...***	***Missing piece***

How would your life change if you filled in the missing pieces that have been stopping you from fully launching yourself in the world?

Look at when and how your missing pieces show up and identify how you can start filling them in. If your mind switches into negative mode as soon as you start thinking about doing something new and scary, then catch it in the act and replace the thought with a positive affirmation based on your missing piece(s) (e.g., I am safe and the universe provides for me). The more you positively reprogramme your system, the more room there is for something new to come in.

Exercise 11

Weigh up the pros and cons of doing each of the activities on your list that you dislike doing. What would you stand to lose if you gave them up? What would you stand to gain?

I would lose...	***I would gain...***

Exercise 12

Imagine that you have only one year to live. What activities would you give up because you considered them a waste of precious time? What would you do instead?

I would give up...	***Instead, I would...***

Your relationship represents a unique forum for self-expression and evolution. In it, you can discover who you are and how to express your unique gifts. If you do not use it for this purpose, it can lose its life-enhancing properties, leaving both partners compromised and unfulfilled. Explore your true self in your relationship and you will find the gifts that you—and the world—have been waiting for.

Chapter 18

Trouble-shooting

This chapter shows you how to recognize the different elements of typical cycles, and how to interrupt them at their various stages of development.

I have not failed. I've just found 10,000 ways that won't work.
—Thomas Alva Edison

Although the techniques and exercises of the 'cycle-busting' process provide the means to break and transform these cycles, deeper levels of consciousness, acceptance, fulfillment and empowerment can always be attained. An ability to troubleshoot keeps us on track with our personal responsibility to achieve our fullest potential. It also reminds us that we are responsible for our issues and for the solutions to our problems.

The symptom	The problem/solution
Arguing over trivial things:	fear of intimacy; resentment over an issue that has not been aired or resolved; dissatisfaction/disappointment as a result of not doing what you love in life, and focusing on petty things as a result; generally unfulfilled in life and, probably, in love. **Solution: talk honestly and openly about the real, underlying source of your unhappiness, allowing all your grief and resentments to come out, and then take some practical, positive steps towards doing what you enjoy.**

The symptom	The problem/solution
Disrespect (leading to arguments or withdrawal):	neither partner is getting his/her needs met and feels out of control of the situation; a lack of personal fulfillment, resulting in unhappiness, for which one's partner is blamed; focusing on one's own needs (i.e., being needy), without consideration for the feelings of the other; fear of confronting or discussing one's issues and instead allowing resentments to build up. **Solution: acknowledge that your partner has been unfairly blamed, and take back responsibility for meeting your own needs. If you are not respecting your partner, respect for yourself is probably also lacking. Work on filling in this missing piece. Disrespect will ultimately destroy your relationship, so you have nothing to lose by addressing your issues and daring to confront them with your partner.**
The silent treatment:	deep resentment over unresolved issues, and unexpressed needs or hurts; feeling misunderstood and unlovable, and that the other person should automatically know and understand your needs; a sense of defeat based on the belief that nothing you say or do will change things. **Solution: dare to express your deepest emotions—honestly and from the heart—no matter what you think the outcome will be. Silence keeps you stuck. Fill in the missing pieces of 'lovability' and powerfulness. If leaving your partner is what you know is required, then you must find the courage to make that move. Practise self-respect so that your choices are based on what is healthy and best for you.**
Anger:	frustration from not getting what you want out of life; feeling powerless or a victim, and needing to blame someone else for the situation; feeling unloved, unimportant, unappreciated or unheard. **Solution: again, identify the missing pieces that relate to your anger, and express yourself honestly and openly to your partner, while filling in these pieces yourself.**

The symptom	The problem/solution
Eating disorders/comfort foods:	a shortage or lack of love and affection; covering up for any issue that you have pushed aside and do not want to face, or cannot stomach; a means of suppressing fear or a sense of inadequacy; a way of dealing with non-specific frustration (as a result of having disconnected from the body and its messages). **Solution: find healthier ways to love and pamper yourself, and make a daily practice of filling in the missing pieces of affection, validation and support. Join a support group and connect with others who will help you reach your personal goals. (See also page 68 for tips on conscious eating.)**
Depression:	the result of suppressed emotions or issues that are important to you; a sense of defeat and a belief that you are powerless to get what you want. **Solution: aerobic movement (in the form of dance or exercise), and deep breathing to bring the emotions to the surface. Once they are accessible, the emotions must be acknowledged. Make a list of what you want and the steps required to get there. Determine your 'missing pieces' and practise filling them in for yourself. Then express yourself as honestly and sincerely as you can. (See Chapter 15: 'Going deeper', for help in accessing buried emotions and bringing a wounded heart back to life.)**
Indecision/confusion:	denial of, or disconnection from, your feelings so that you are unable to make a true choice based on what you want; knowing what you want to do but too afraid to do it and second-guessing yourself as a result. **Solution: trust your gut instinct. Confusion always results when you know what you must do but your fears prevent you from doing it. Examine your fears and weigh them against the disadvantages of acting against your better judgement. Ignoring your intuition usually backfires.**

The symptom	The problem/solution
Loss of sexual appetite:	(in the absence of any physical ailment/condition and in the presence of genuine love for your partner) unresolved hurts or emotions that have generated sadness or resentment; a lack of trust based on abuse (past or present), disrespect or insensitivity; a lack of communication, leading to an emotional distancing or a failure to connect with one's heart; needs or expectations of one's partner, which can create a sense of obligation for the other, leading to resentment and an emotional shut-down. **Solution:** **1) sensual reconnection. This is not necessarily about sex, but sensuality and the re-awakening of the body and the heart through the senses. This involves asking for what you want from your partner, in terms of sensual and/or sexual fulfillment, and also taking care of your own needs in this area, by loving yourself in physical and emotional ways. See 'Re-awakening the body' in Chapter 15.** **2) honest communication. This requires honesty and commitment from both parties. See 'Clearing the way to better communication' in Chapter 15 for ways to clear unresolved issues and express your deepest feelings in a safe environment. This is a powerful way to generate intimacy.**

Chapter 19

The 10 commitments:
a code of consciousness for a fulfilling life

The following 10 principles constitute a condensed code for maintaining one's spiritual consciousness and an awareness of one's personal power. It is designed to help you stay on track with your purpose, your power, your unconditional acceptance and your love.

1. I make conscious choices in every moment—responding to that moment, rather than reacting to the past. I listen to and respect my inner voice and my body, and I make my choices accordingly.

2. I allow myself to be uniquely and authentically me—not a clone of, or a reaction to, someone else. I dare to be me, regardless of how it might affect others (as long as I do not harm them).

3. I use my power wisely and consciously, aware of its impact on the world. I am mindful of what I say and think, how I act and project, and how I present myself to others.

4. I know, accept, respect and love myself, retaining my identity in all relationships.

5. I remind myself not to let the 'drama' or circumstances of life distract me from the real source of my problems and solutions—me.

6. I see myself in all others, and I see my relationships with others as a vehicle for mutual growth—a sounding board, and a yardstick of my personal power.

7. I trust myself, knowing that I am always taken care of, and that the biggest insult to God or the universe is to worry. The biggest insult to myself is to fall short of my potential because of fear or self-doubt.

8. I am committed to loving in the face of lovelessness. I dare to look for the love and good in all others, despite what they may appear to be on the outside.

9. I treat myself and others the way I would want to be treated. I am gentle with myself and my temporary limitations, and am gentle with others also, allowing them to be the way they are, without judgement.

10. I focus on being happy, rather than on being right.

Notes